PUBLISH TO SELL

LONG TERM INCOME
FROM SHORT TERM EFFORT

ALEX GOLDSTEIN

Publish To Sell: Long Term Income from Short Term Effort

© 2014 Alex Goldstein PLLC

All rights reserved. No part of this publication may be printed, reproduced, stored in a retrieval system, or transmitted, emailed, uploaded in any form or by any means, electronic, mechanical photocopying, recording, or otherwise, without the prior written permission of the publisher.

This publication is sold with the understanding that neither the author or the publisher is engaged in rendering legal, accounting, financial or other professional service. If legal advice or other expert assistance is required, the services of a competent professional person should be sought.

ISBN-13: 978-1500592295
ISBN-10: 1500592293

TABLE OF CONTENTS

How I Made $70,000 by Accident 1
Get Paid 10 Years… 9
…for Just a Week's Work 15
How to Go Broke Publishing a Bestseller 21
Still Not Convinced You Should Publish a Book? 31
How to Sell More to People Who Have Not Read Your Book 37
Never Discount Again 41
What If I've Already Started My Book? 49
The BCOOL Solution 53
Brainstorm Part I 61
   Planning Your Book is Like Learning to Survive a Bear Attack
Brainstorm Part II 65
   Step by Step
Brainstorm Part III 81
   The Most Important Page in Your Book
Brainstorm Part IV 89
   Attention Ikea Shoppers
Create Part I 93
   Writing by the Pound
Create Part II 99
   Step by Step

Create Part III 105
    You Are Now an Inventor
Create Part IV 115
    The Mighty, Mighty Table of Contents
Organize 121
Outsource 127
Launch 135
Afterword 143
    The Biggest Mistake You Can Make—and How to Avoid It
Bonuses for Readers 147
Acknowledgements 149
About the Author 153

HOW I MADE $70,000 BY ACCIDENT

I'd rather be lucky than smart.
~ Donald Luskin, investor and Yale dropout

I made $70,000 by accident. When I told friends the surprising story of how it happened, they told me I had to teach them or they wouldn't be my friends anymore. In essence, I was compelled to write this book. It wasn't part of my life plan.

Here's how this unusual, true story began:

I started working as a real estate agent and was looking for ways to generate new business. So I wrote an e-book about how people could buy a home without any bank financing. It was at a time shortly after the housing crash, prices were low, sellers were desperate, and buyers couldn't get financing. I had some knowledge in this area and thought it would help people. I wrote what I knew, paid someone $100 to make a pretty layout in a PDF, and started running some ads on Craigslist to build my email list. I had added only about 200 emails to my list when Craigslist shut me down.

Apparently, I was violating Craigslist's terms of service, and I didn't even know it. I tried to figure out what I did wrong, then I tried to hire a Craigslist consultant. I went through about six so-called experts and ultimately concluded it wasn't worth the aggravation. The market had changed, and housing prices were up. The e-book didn't seem relevant anymore, so I stopped marketing it.

This was just one of many episodes of "roller coaster marketing" in which a strategy delivered exciting results, and then all of a sudden let me down. I had tried many different ways to market my business, and it was usually a ride up, and then a ride down just as quickly. When I pushed and cajoled, I got results—sometimes. Other times, something would change beyond my control and I was back to square one. I just wanted something that I could setup once, and would work for a long time without requiring my attention.

As luck would have it, I had already created the long-term solution without even knowing it. A couple of years later, I was reviewing my transactions and was shocked to realize that I had generated $70,000 in recent commissions as a direct result of the e-book. Over time, a handful of people had found the book, read it and sought me out. It wasn't a lot of people. But they were the *right* people—motivated clients who wanted to buy what I was selling. So the e-book that I had all but forgotten about—and hadn't spent a nickel promoting in years—delivered me some of my best clients. The book made the sale, not me. People read the book and they were convinced they had to do business with me. The conversation usually went along the lines of: "I read your book; it was very helpful. How do we get started together?"

Crazy as it may sound, I was actually annoyed when I saw these results. I had spent a lot of money on other forms of marketing, including direct mail and online advertising. Beyond the money, these methods required a lot of my time to manage all the moving parts. They generated a lot of unqualified prospects, and so I spent a lot of time qualifying people and wasting energy on folks who didn't respect my time. So I found myself annoyed by how hard I had been working and how much energy I had expended to get the same result I got from something that hadn't taken an ounce of effort in years: my book.

After I got over my frustration, I accepted that some of my money was not as hard-earned as the rest, and decided to learn from the experience. I wanted more success of the same kind: lucrative clients who respect my expertise and follow my advice.

> There are two traits I have seen in all my best clients, and in those clients served by my colleagues and students as well. They are:
>
> 1. **Profitable**—These clients bring in a lot of revenue and are often 10 times more valuable than the average client.
>
> 2. **Implementors**—These clients implement the advice you give them. They take action instead of asking endless questions. They work on your terms and your schedule, and as a result they achieve great results.
>
> I call these wonderful people **PI Clients—Profitable Implementors**. The more PI Clients you have in your life, the better your life will be.

After the success of my first book, I wrote another. The book targeted a different market segment (luxury real estate) and with a different format (Kindle and paperback instead of PDF). I also peppered this book with "celebrity" associations and used an interview format. Importantly, this second book incorporated the lessons learned from my first book, to make it more successful than most of its kind. Lo and behold, the second book also had a superb return on investment: six figures and counting.

Yet something very important happened *before* this book had time to deliver revenue from new clients. It isn't feasible to generate a lot of new revenue quickly in luxury real estate because it is inherently a long sales cycle. People need time to make decisions and close transactions. What happened quickly, though, is that I started getting business calls from people I already knew, but who hadn't done business with me previously. People who had known me for years perceived me differently after I published my book.

Furthermore, friends and associates also started to refer to me far more frequently when the subject of real estate came up in their everyday conversations. You can tell people what you do for a living, but it usually goes in one ear and out the other. You get the polite nod or the brief conversation. However, it's an entirely different situation when you hand them a signed copy of your paperback. That doesn't happen every day, and people remember it. They now know what you do, they perceive you as an expert, and they remember you the next time your area of expertise comes up in their lives.

Once I had two totally different marketing approaches for the same business (traditional advertising and books), I began to see patterns. The most important of these was that the clients who read the book were different from those who hadn't. I saw differences in my working relationships with clients who had read the book. Clients who came from my books were easy to work with, listened to me, and valued my advice. I also received my full fee; discounting either never came up or was quickly ruled out.

Clearly, writing these books was the best thing I had done for my business, not only putting money in my pocket, but also improving my lifestyle. It's one thing to make more money, but it's so much better when you actually enjoy your work. Clients who work on your terms and follow your advice can make just about any job fun.

With this knowledge, I knew I wanted to write a third book about real estate. However, real estate book number three hasn't happened yet—because of the book you are reading right now. My friends and associates begged me: "I want to publish a book for my financial planning/real estate/coaching/you-name-it business and get the results you got! How do I do it?" I started blabbing, and they said, "No! I want the complete method step by step. Write it down please—*now*."

Given their almost rabid enthusiasm, I agreed to give them what they wanted. And that is the story of how this book came to be. The methods in this book are broadly applicable. They've been implemented successfully not only in residential real estate but in many other industries.

> This book has one objective and one objective only: to show you how to quickly publish your own book that will deliver PI Clients for many years to come.

Who this book is for:

- People who sell high-value products and services.
- People seeking a marketing method that will deliver results for many years to come, as an alternative to "flavor-of-the-month" marketing strategies that are useful for only a short time.
- People who understand their marketing is an investment, and carefully monitor the return on that investment.
- People who want clients to begin working with them already knowing—and agreeing with—how they do business.
- People who want a long-term asset, one that consistently generates clients for years and doesn't require constant "care and feeding."

Who this book is *not* for:

- People who sell low-value, mass merchandise, commodity products or services. This book was written with high-value products and services in mind, and that's where these techniques have been tested. They may not work in other areas. However, one exception may be if your product or service actually has a lot of value, but is *perceived* as having low value. In that case, the techniques in this book can be extremely effective to change that perception.
- People who don't take action. This book is about *quickly* publishing a book that delivers PI Clients. If you don't apply what's in this book, it will get no results for you. The key is *doing* something, not thinking about it.
- People who do not invest in themselves or their business. If you spend all your effort minimizing costs and don't try to maximize your return on investment, then the techniques in this book will not be effective for you.

- People who believe that difficult clients, constant interruptions, and long hours are "just the way it is" and that it's impossible to change that.
- People who don't care whether their clients get results and who just want to get paid. If you don't genuinely care about your clients and the results they get, no marketing method or sales technique can transform your business.

This book does not aspire to be all things to all people. But it will be highly effective for people who apply the methods contained herein. The chapters that follow will guide you through how to quickly author and publish a book that will deliver PI Clients year after year and grow your business.

Summary

- Your book, when properly structured, is your best salesperson. It will close the deal, not just generate leads.

- PI (Profitable Implementor) Clients are the people we want to attract. Write to them and for them, and don't worry about anyone else.

- Step off the marketing roller coaster and get consistent long-term results. Your book will deliver PI Clients for many years to come, and will be an asset to you and your business, regardless of the latest marketing fads.

GET PAID 10 YEARS...

I very frequently get the question: 'What's going to change in the next 10 years?' And that is a very interesting question; it's a very common one. I almost never get the question: 'What's not going to change in the next 10 years?' And I submit to you that that second question is actually the more important of the two... When you have something that you know is true, even over the long term, you can afford to put a lot of energy into it.
~ Jeff Bezos, CEO of Amazon

We live in a world obsessed with the newest, latest, and greatest. We've seen many mighty institutions crumble in the past ten years as the pace of change has accelerated. Facebook has a billion users, but will it in ten years? It wasn't long ago that MySpace was a juggernaut with more than 100 million users, and then it faded into oblivion.

Books, however, have been around for thousands of years. The way they are produced has changed, but the structure is pretty much the same. It's a safe bet that ten years from now, books will still be around. There will probably be more of them in electronic format and fewer in paper. People may read less in ten years and watch more video. But most people will still read, and will have respect for authors.

What's even more important than what "most" people do is what's done by the people we want to reach. This book is about selling high-value products and services, things obtainable by only people who have some wealth. We don't know exactly what the wealthy will be doing in ten years, but there are currently some pretty major differences between the wealthy and "most people," and those are likely to persist.

In 2014, here's what we know about the reading habits of rich versus poor:

- 88% of the wealthy read 30 minutes or more each day versus 2% of the poor.
- 63% of the wealthy listened to audio books during their commute to work versus 5% of the poor.
- The books wealthy people read disproportionately include non-fiction books, such as history, self-help, science, career-related, educational books and biographies.[1]

The techniques in this book are designed to sell high-value services, so we want to know what the rich are doing and meet them where they are. The good news is the rich are still reading, and it's reasonable to project that they will be in ten years—and probably 20, 30, 40, or 50 years. Compare this to most Internet marketing techniques, and

---

[1] Source: http://richhabits.net/is-there-a-correlation-between-being-rich-and-reading-habits/

even television and radio—consumer habits are constantly shifting, and the competitive landscape can be ruthless.

We know that books will be around for many years to come and that wealthy people will continue to read them. If you embrace writing and publishing as a marketing technique for your high-value services, you're investing in something that you *know* will pay dividends for many years to come. Books are not MySpace or some other wonder technology with fifteen minutes of fame. Publishing is a long-term strategy—an increasingly rare thing in today's world of rapid change.

If you have already mastered other marketing and advertising techniques, your book will multiply their effectiveness. You don't need to choose between them. Rather, they all work well together and can produce better results combined than any could do on their own. Your book enhances your other advertising and marketing channels, so you can get better results with less expense and effort.

Most books are written with the sole purpose of selling lots of copies. Consequently, an author's "success" is valued only in the number of books sold, which has nothing to do with profitability. A book using the techniques in Publish to Sell, however, has only one goal: to deliver PI Clients for years to come. Fortunately, you do not have to author a bestseller and sell hundreds of thousands of copies to achieve that goal.

When people consider writing a book, they are often intimidated by the writing process. They think they don't have the knowledge, skill or time to complete the task. The publishing industry stokes these fears with a lot of yammering about bestsellers and branding. As a result, too many businesspeople erroneously believe authoring a book is a hard task with an uncertain payoff. That is absolutely false, as long as you use the correct approach. This book will demystify the process, and get you rapid results.

Many people are also intimidated by the production process. They don't know how to physically publish a book, and believe it's an onerous task. That was a valid point some years ago, but it's no longer true. Today, Amazon and several other companies have transformed publishing, making it astonishingly cheap and easy for people to publish books. And publishing is only going to get better, faster, easier and cheaper in years to come. The skills you learn will only become more valuable with time.

If you are currently selling high-value products or services, then I promise you that you *can* author and publish a book that *will* be an effective long-term tool for delivering PI Clients. We will not cover how to sell to the mass market, nor will we discuss how to write The Great American Novel. This book has one purpose: to get you on the quickest path to a book that generates PI Clients for you, year after year.

Summary

- Jeff Bezos runs one of the world's most successful companies by asking, "What's not going to change in 10 years?" You should run your business that way, too.

- 88% of the wealthy read thirty minutes or more each day versus 2% of the poor. Meet your prosperous customers where they are, with a book.

- You do not need to sell a lot of copies of a book to make a lot of money. A few PI Clients are worth a hundred mediocre clients.

- Your book will multiply the effectiveness of your existing marketing and sales efforts. You don't have to choose between them—you can grow them all at the same time.

...FOR JUST A WEEK'S WORK

Motion beats meditation.
~ GARY HALBERT, COPYWRITER

Most people are highly skeptical that a book can be produced in a week, let alone be any good. Here's the secret: we're not finishing the *book* in a week, just the *manuscript*. Your work as the author is conceiving your idea and giving birth to it on paper.

Everything that happens from the creation of that initial manuscript to the point the book is finished—editing, layout, artwork, and printing—will involve the work and expertise of other people. These experts can be hired quickly, and at a reasonable cost. The part that depends upon you, the author, does not take more than a week's time, if you follow the process detailed in this book.

A work week for most people is 40 hours. You can write a *lot* in that much time, certainly enough for a manuscript. If you are speaking your book—either dictating it or being interviewed—you could speak a *stack* of books in 40 hours. Most people spend many months wasting time because they are looking at a blank page with fear. They have no process, and yet they also expect perfection, so they are bound to fail. In sum, they think that just sitting down and typing is all they have to do to make magic happen.

The process in this book will help you structure your thinking so that when you sit down to write, you already know what's going to be there. There is no fear of the blank page when you use this process. Just by answering questions, you're going to produce ideas and information that are extremely valuable to the reader and that give your effort momentum.

It's critically important to know that not all authors are writers. If writing scares you, then it's perfectly acceptable to speak your book. Several hours of dictated thoughts can be transcribed very cheaply. You can then pay an editor or ghostwriter to collaborate with you and weave your thoughts into a book. There is no shame in this whatsoever. Virtually every celebrity autobiography has been done in exactly this fashion. If it's good enough for movie stars, it's good enough for you.

Should you choose to dictate your book—or be interviewed or use a ghostwriter—the process in this book remains the same and will be just as effective. Imagine if you spent four hours rambling on a recording without any clue of what you wanted to say or why. You could hardly expect the end result to be spun gold. The methods in this book will ensure that speaking your book will be productive and result in a quality book.

The simple truth is this: THE BOOK IS ALREADY IN YOUR BRAIN, YOU JUST HAVE TO GET IT OUT. The subject you are writing about is something you know. It's something you've done for years. You have experience in your field, and that experience has yielded expertise. That expertise will be the heart of your book.

Sometimes people are not confident in their own expertise, but when they start the process in this book, they are pleasantly surprised by how much they actually know. Read on, and you'll have an easy blueprint to quickly get the book out of your brain and into print.

The critical difference between publishing to sell and publishing for literary or artistic value is that casual, plain language is *essential*. The objective is to persuade people about your industry, product, or service. You can't persuade people if they don't understand what you're saying.

The trouble comes when we don't give ourselves a deadline. Sure, you can stretch writing out for years if you want. But taking longer doesn't necessarily make a book any better, certainly not the type of book that we are writing. In all likelihood, it makes it worse. How could a book written in a week be better than one written in a year, you may ask? The answer is plain language.

We can spend all the time in the world making something more complicated than it needs to be. This is not only more painful for you, the author, it's also more painful for the reader, and thus for your wallet. Simple language that clearly explains your point is what's important. If you write quickly, you don't have time to complicate your thoughts. If you write conversationally—writing like you speak—it will be easy for the reader to understand.

Please banish images from your mind of the tortured author, working for years in a remote cabin, ripping up draft after draft in between tearing out chunks of her own hair. That author has as much in common with us as a fish has with a dog. We are different creatures, from different environments, with different goals—and therefore we have entirely different behavior.

When we pull back the curtain, we see that the fear of writing being a long and complicated process is overblown for several critical reasons:

- **Once you have a manuscript, it's a slam dunk to get to the finished book that will generate PI Clients for your business.** The first week is all that requires your focus; it's about *your* ideas. After that, you will have experienced professionals helping you through the rest of the process. This book, and the free resources on the *Publish to Sell* website, will help you be successful.
- **Speaking is just as productive as writing.** Most celebrity autobiographies written in recent decades were not "written" by the author at all. Rather, someone interviewed them and put their words into a narrative format. You can pay someone to do this for you and quickly generate content for your book. For the most current resources on being an author without ever writing, download "How to Be an Author Without Writing" at **NoWriting.PublishToSell.Com.**
- **The table of contents is half the battle.** Writing (or speaking) your manuscript without a table of contents is like going on a long road trip, to a place you've never been, with no map. You may get there eventually, but it will be painful and frustrating. Later in this book, we'll cover the creation of a table of contents.
- **You're not authoring The Great American Novel.** There's nothing that you need to dream up; you are simply putting on paper what is already in your brain. Once you get started, you'll be amazed at how much you have to say and how quickly you can get it on the page.

- **Perfection isn't the goal. Getting PI Clients quickly, and for many years to come, is the goal.** The reason that many people who start writing a book never finish it is because they get obsessed with perfection. Perfection doesn't exist, and the book that is never released is guaranteed to get you zero results. That's why it's important to commit to serious deadlines and to trust the process. Once you follow the steps, you'll have an effective book. If you want to revise the book in the future, that's easy to do. Getting the first version out the door is what matters.

Summary

- Writing faster is better. Completing the manuscript is more important than anything else. An editor can do wonders even with the roughest manuscript.

- The techniques in this book will make sure that you know exactly what to do by the time you write or speak your manuscript.

- The book is already in your brain, we just have to get it out. You are writing about a subject you already know well. It's not the Great American Novel, there's no plot or character to dream up. We simply have to extract and organize.

HOW TO GO BROKE PUBLISHING A BESTSELLER

What's the best way to make a small fortune?
Start with a large fortune and buy a boat.
~ ANONYMOUS

There is one guiding principle that will help you make all of your publishing decisions: does it deliver PI Clients? If the answer is yes, then let's do it. If the answer is no, then it's unnecessary and may even be counterproductive.

> **Rule #1:** Does it deliver PI Clients?
>
> **Rule #2:** If I get PI Clients, do I really need another rule?

Please pay close attention to the language of Rule #1. *Deliver* means they're ready to get to work, the book has made the sale and you're essentially just an order taker by the time they contact you. *PI Clients* mean a lucrative and enjoyable outcome. They pay your rates, implement your advice, and get great results.

Here are some of the things Rule #1 does *not* say:

- Write a bestseller
- Build celebrity
- Build branding
- Generate leads
- Get speaking gigs

You may be thinking that all of the above looks pretty good, and why wouldn't we shoot for these goals, too? It is quite possible that some or all of this will happen as a side effect of our efforts; however, we cannot effectively serve many masters and be successful. In the words of the philosopher Publius Syrus: "To do two things at once is to do neither." Let's focus on authoring a book that will deliver PI Clients, because that's money in our pockets. Anything else that happens will be a bonus.

> Always remember: you can't spell Bestseller without B.S.

The enemy of the PI Client way of thinking is the Bestseller Mentality—which I cheerfully refer to as the BS Mentality herein. This is a set of beliefs that fuels fears about writing and publishing, and prevents people from taking action. Here are some examples:

BS Mentality: Sell a lot of books and the profits will follow.
PI Client Mentality: A small number of PI Clients will maximize profit and fun, while minimizing cost and hassle. You can

generate phenomenal revenue from PI Clients without selling a lot of books. The desire to sell a lot of books is a distraction that can lead to frustration and failure.

BS Mentality: Sell a lot of copies and a book can be an additional income stream.
PI Client Mentality: There are thousands of people who work full time in book promotion. Most of them make peanuts. Trying to make big money promoting books as an extra income is a distraction and a headache. The real money comes from adding additional income to the business you already have.

BS Mentality: If you don't sell a lot of books, then readers won't take the book seriously.
PI Client Mentality: Every person in the world cares more about themselves than whatever is important to you. If the book speaks to their specific desires and needs, they *will* have an interest in the book and the author. How many copies a book has sold is totally irrelevant to the reader, provided the material inside helps them. **Remember the two R's: Reader Results. If your book provides amazing results to for the reader, your book *will* be successful.**

BS Mentality: Books can lead to speaking engagements and other new income streams.
PI Client Mentality: It's a diversion to build other income streams before you've maximized the one you already have. There are enough moving parts in the process of writing, publishing, and promoting a book. Don't add to your plate before your book is even finished. *Publish to Sell* will simplify the process and focus on one result, and one result only: delivering PI Clients to your existing business.

BS Mentality: Build your brand to build your profits.
PI Client Mentality: You can't make a mortgage payment with a brand.

BS Mentality: Bestselling books prove your credibility.
PI Client Mentality: This may have been true a decade ago, but with every passing year it becomes less meaningful. There's a whole industry around gaming the system to create "bestselling" books. Anyone can write a check and have a bestseller tomorrow. Some brazen folks are literally buying thousands of copies of their own book to get on a bestseller list. Also, thousands of authors are coming up with ever more creative definitions of "bestseller"—#1 in the category of llama farming in Texas for 15 minutes on Amazon, here's a screenshot! As P.T. Barnum said, you can't fool all the people all the time. The secret is out: everyone and their cousin is a bestselling author.

We are on a specific mission, and as long as we keep our guiding principle in mind—delivering PI Clients—then we have a compass by which to orient all of our efforts. So whenever you may be in doubt about anything you're doing in the writing, publishing, or promotion of your book, ask yourself this: does it support delivering PI Clients?

Being a bestselling author doesn't mean much, unless you are a legitimate phenomenon like the author of the Harry Potter series, J. K. Rowling. For the rest of us, focusing on the reader's self-interest is a hundred times more powerful—and profitable—than how many copies a book has sold.

> *It's difficult to get a man to understand something when his salary depends on his not understanding it.*
> ~ UPTON SINCLAIR, AUTHOR

The small-but-profitable mentality flies in the face of most of the publishing industry. That's because most of the publishing industry isn't trying to sell high-value products and services. They are trying to mass market books. Most of the publishing industry is appealing to egos; getting famous and sticking it to the people who said you'd never amount to anything is appealing to millions of people.

> The biggest dirty secret of the publishing industry is that a small-but-profitable business model would bankrupt them. They need volume to profit. If a traditional publisher sold just 500 copies of a book, it's a huge loss for them. You, however, can make a phenomenal profit selling high value products and services from just 500 copies of a book. The traditional publishing industry cannot accommodate you. However, the self-publishing revolution is an epic gift for entrepreneurs.

For all the reasons above, please banish BS Mentality from your brain, and let's move forward with gusto.

It should be pretty obvious to any business owner that no marketing method has a 100% conversion rate. So, our effort cannot hope to turn 100% of readers into clients. We will also produce some leads and prospects that don't turn into clients, it's inevitable. Please remember that **we are not trying to generate leads, we are trying to deliver PI Clients—and whenever the two may conflict, sacrifice the former to focus on the latter.**

So how can your book actually deliver PI Clients? When someone reads the book and has this reaction: "I hope this author will accept my money, because I *have* to work with him/her."

It takes more to deliver a PI Client than to deliver a lead. Therefore, just as we are deliberately putting things in the book to appeal to the best prospects, we are also inserting material that will repel the worst prospects. In other words, we are willing to reduce the number of leads to increase the number of PI Clients.

If you only get two clients from publishing a book, and they are each worth $50,000 to your business—and you never receive any other phone calls—then your book has made a massive return on investment. Think about it: you got $100,000 in revenue, you didn't have to spend a ton of time and energy with lousy prospects, and you got a fantastic return on your time and money.

The reality is that you will generate a lot more than two clients. Your book is out there permanently, it's on people's shelves and on their smartphones. That alone will result in people calling you out of the blue.

Furthermore, you can promote your book whenever you want, and improve its ability to deliver more clients. Contrast this with the BS Mentality, which creates a huge drama around the book launch. BS Mentality tells you that the book either succeeds or fails in the first days after publication. That may be true if you care about getting on a list in a newspaper. However, we only care about delivering PI Clients.

You don't need an extravagant launch, and you don't need a red carpet event. You can promote the book anytime you want, and drum up more clients anytime you want. Just hit the gas on your promotional efforts as much or as little as necessary to deliver the number of clients your business can handle. Of course, your book has to be written to attract PI Clients in the first place.

> For your book to deliver PI Clients, you must be willing to repel the wrong person as much as you are willing to attract the right person.

For example, let's think about the book in your hand. I did some things that are bound to offend or repel some people. For example, in this book I state:

- **I'm expensive.** While I would love to be able to help everyone personally, there is only so much time. I won't help anyone other than PI Clients. Someone who is looking for a cheap, quick fix should not contact me. I only work with people who invest massively in their businesses to get a high return on investment.
- **Many people want to write a book to build their brand or get speaking engagements, and I specifically state that my methods are not targeting those things.** People who follow my methods have great opportunities to build their brand and get speaking gigs, but that's just a side-effect. Instead, I advocate staying focused on the prize: PI Clients.
- **I'm choosy about my clients. I won't just take anyone's money.** If someone has a bad attitude or is a procrastinator, it doesn't matter how much money they're willing to pay me. I got into this to enjoy my life, and no amount of money is worth not enjoying it.
- **I don't make pie-in-the-sky promises.** If someone's business is broken, if they are not creating value for their customers, I don't tell them that a book is going to fix that. I'm not going to be someone's "Hail Mary" play to save a business that's hopeless.

Those ideas are going to repel some people. But that's okay because I'm not trying to work with people who have goals that run contrary to mine. I'm making very clear the types of people who will benefit from working with me, and those who will not.

When someone is done reading your book, they should have a clear picture whether they can or should work with you. Some will detest you after reading the book, and that's okay. They'd never be clients anyway, and there's no point trying to cajole them. Focus instead on the people who will read your book and hear the bells go off. Concentrate on the PI Clients who will come calling because what they read made absolute sense—and they are hungry for more.

To conclude, *Publish to Sell* is about generating the best clients—the clients we'll enjoy, who work on our terms, and who are happy to pay for the privilege. Any other effects, such as speaking engagements or fame, are to be considered happy byproducts. Weeding out the people who are a wrong fit is just as important as delivering the people who are a right fit. We are attracting *and* repelling in order to achieve our goal of delivering PI Clients.

Summary

- You can't spell Bestseller without B.S.—so we call it the BS Mentality. There's a whole lot of BS Mentality in the publishing industry, making people believe they need to sell a zillion copies to be successful. You can make a *lot* of money from just a few readers becoming PI Clients.

- The BS Mentality is dangerous because it overcomplicates the process, fuels doubts and risks making people give up along the way. If you focus on profitability instead of traditional publishing metrics, you'll make money much faster and easier than the BS Mentality would ever permit.

- To deliver a PI Client, you must be willing to repel the wrong person in order to attract the right person.

STILL NOT CONVINCED YOU SHOULD PUBLISH A BOOK?

The customer who comes from one of my books is a substantially more valuable customer than those who arrive through any other means.
~ Dan Kennedy, copywriter

In addition to delivering PI Clients, there are other benefits of taking action immediately and publishing your book:

Your Business Strategy Will Be Clearer than Ever
Virtually all my clients have told me they dramatically improved their business strategy, *before* they even started to write the first page of their manuscript. The techniques in this book include a structured method of thinking to help you better understand your business, your beliefs, and your role in your industry. Not only will this process make your book successful, it can solve problems that may have been nagging at you for years. *Publish to Sell* forces you to answer seri-

ous questions, and consequently your strategy will be as clear and durable as a polished diamond.

Your Employees Will Be Happier and More Productive

Communication could use major improvement in almost every business. Think of how many times clients and customers interact with the lowest-paid employees of a business, and form their opinions about the business right then and there. And yet, how often do bosses communicate their vision for the company to *all* employees? And how effective is that communication?

Usually the boss thinks it should be obvious what the employees should do, and how they should behave. However, sometimes employees literally don't know what to do, so they improvise and stumble. It's the boss's fault that the communication has broken down. Your book will ensure that your employees clearly understand your vision, enabling them to make better decisions and be more productive.

Also, your employees will be proud to work for an author. Everyone wants to be able to brag about their job, and it's a lot easier to do that when they're working for an author. A book is a big deal to many people, it's exciting. Your assistant is more likely to tell his/her friends he/she works for an author than a lawyer, financial advisor, consultant, real estate agent, or whatever title you may now use. Employees that are proud to work for you are going to be happier and more productive.

Your Book Can Open Global Markets

Let's imagine that you and one of your competitors want to do business for the first time in England. Who is better positioned to make that happen: the author that sends his/her book to prospective partners, or the salesperson who has to convince everyone from scratch on every phone call?

Your Book Has Billions of Dollars Behind It

Amazon spent tens of billions of dollars building and promoting a distribution platform for you. You get access to this world-class system free, and the cost to print books on demand is cheaper than it's ever been. And, thanks to the wonders of the Internet, you have access to any army of capable and affordable editors, artists and layout hands to help along the way.

It's an absolutely incredible time to be self-publishing a book.

You Can Reduce Compliance Problems With Marketing

Do you work in an industry that is highly regulated? Are bureaucrats sucking the soul out of your marketing efforts and watering down your message to the point of being totally ineffective? A book can help solve that problem.

You may not be able to promote your medical services or financial advisory the way you'd like, but you can promote your book with great vigor and creativity. Savvy doctors, financial advisors, lawyers, and others in industries burdened with "red tape" have used books to build their businesses. Provide valuable information to the marketplace and you will get PI Clients.

Books Will Never Go Out of Style

The latest social media fads will quickly come and go. Remember MySpace? It conquered the world—then disappeared. Books have been around for thousands of years. People will still respect books and their authors in years to come, regardless of whether they read them. This is critical: even if people never read your book, your reputation will benefit from having written it.

Clients Will Do Business On Your Terms

A book allows you to convey all the nuances of how you work. It explains the results clients should expect, what clients should do to get those results, and what behavior is not acceptable. When people work with you after reading your book, they know your value and how you do business. You cannot build this kind of deep relationship with a stranger using a tweet, or a three page sales letter.

Your Book Never Sleeps

Your book is building credibility 24 hours a day, seven days a week. It's on people's shelves, in their tablets, and on their phones. Years after you've written it, someone somewhere will be learning about you and benefitting from the value you've provided.

Your book is an asset that can continue to deliver cash and customers years after you've published it. Even if you haven't promoted your book in a year (or in my case, years), it can still deliver superb clients. How many other marketing programs continue to deliver new business years after you've created them, with little or no maintenance?

You Will Make Life Miserable for Your Competitors

With whom would you rather have a conversation: a salesperson or a published author? Very few people will ever write a book in their lives—and that includes the folks you compete against. Those of your competitors who write a book without the techniques in *Publish to Sell* will likely make numerous mistakes, failing to deliver the results you will enjoy.

Summary

Your book has several compelling benefits far beyond what most people understand:

- Employees will be more effective and happier.
- Your business strategy will be clearer than ever.
- Clients will do business on your terms.
- Your competition will be left in the dust.
- Global markets can be opened more effectively.
- Books work for the long term, they're not a fad.

HOW TO SELL MORE TO PEOPLE WHO HAVE NOT READ YOUR BOOK

You never get a second chance to make a good first impression.
~ WILL ROGERS, ACTOR

When someone you've never met before asks what you do, what's the best possible answer?

It's a trick question. There are three answers, all of which are equally correct: movie star, professional athlete, and rock star. The person who can honestly give one of those answers is going to have people very, very interested. They are going to be listened to very carefully. They are going to get some perks.

For the rest of us, the script is usually different. This is how things typically go:

Question: What do you do?
Answer: I'm a real estate agent.

What They're Thinking: I know 26 of them in my town, and 25 of them are mad when I don't work with them. I need to anger a 26th person like I need a hole in my head.
What They Say: Nice meeting you.

Question: What do you do?
Answer: I'm in technology sales.
What They're Thinking: I had better cut this short before they start talking about gigabytes or synergy.
What They Say: Cool.

Question: What do you do?
Answer: I'm a lawyer.
What They're Thinking: That reminds me of the time I got sued. Ugh.
What They Say: Oh, I have a nephew in law school.

Question: What do you do?
Answer: I'm an accountant.
What They're Thinking: Is there anything more boring?
What They Say: Oh, terrific.

Any of the people in the professions above could have a different conversation if they choose. They could have this conversation instead:

Question: What do you do?
Answer: I'm an author.
What They're Thinking: Wish I was an author.
What They Say: Oh really? What's your book about?

From there, you can say real estate, law, or probably navel gazing and you'll be a lot more interesting than the person next to you.

How to Sell More to People Who Have Not Read Your Book

Now you may be thinking, "But Alex, you told me it's all about the sales, who cares about being interesting?" Conversations like this *are* sales.

Perhaps you're someone who has never quite felt comfortable "working a room." If you don't initiate relationships when opportunity knocks, then you're like a batter who's been sitting on the bench. It doesn't matter how skilled you are, if you don't even get a chance to swing. Being an author is like having the coach call you off the bench to go to the plate. Sometimes you'll hit it out of the park, and sometimes you'll strike out. What's important is you improve your skills every time at bat.

Sales is a process, and the first step is getting people's attention. So the beauty of being an author is that someone who's never even read your book—and maybe never will—is still willing to walk a few steps down the road to a sale with you.

It works for referrals, too. To get a referral, people need to know what you do and why you're better than your competitors. In casual conversations, your job or business typically goes in one ear and out the other. But when you say "author" the dynamic is different, and people pay more attention. You will have more meaningful conversations, and you'll have an easy method of follow-up: "I'd be happy to send you a copy of my book if you'd like to read it?"

You don't have to believe me, just try it. Once you have produced a book where you've taken a stand and you've risked making some people angry, you *will* have something interesting to talk about. You'll stand tall when someone asks you what you do, and you say, "I'm an author."

Summary

- Being an author is more interesting, and sparks more conversation, than most job titles. Use that to your advantage to build your business and your relationships every time you walk into a room.

- Books are a great tool to generate referrals. You're giving people a gift, and they'll remember who you are and what you do.

- The first time someone asks you what you do and you say, "I'm an author" you will be hooked for life. Enjoy it, and prosper from it.

NEVER DISCOUNT AGAIN

What we obtain too cheap, we esteem too lightly: it is dearness only that gives every thing its value.
~ Thomas Paine, Founding Father of the U.S.A.

It's inevitable that someone is going to ask for your services at a discount. On the one hand, you can't blame them for trying, right? On the other hand, this is a bad sign that they'll probably be a pain in the behind.

Of course you want to say, "Hell No!" to discounts, but part of you may not have the guts to stonewall a client. Maybe you want to finesse the situation and can't figure out how. Maybe you lose your nerve. Whatever the case, help is here.

It's critical to stop this sort of bad behavior immediately, and if you can't, then part ways with the client. The key is to rip off the Band-Aid; don't peel it off slowly. Do it quickly and either resolve the problem or move on.

Your book is a great tool for dealing with discounters. Anyone who has read your book should be aware of the value you bring to the table and the type of behavior you will and will not tolerate.

Remember, when you have literally written the book on the subject, you have tremendous power to protect the integrity of your pricing. Prospects who have read your book will want you, and only you. It would be extremely difficult for a competitor to get the same level of respect in your marketplace.

Here is how I dealt with readers of my first real estate book who were seeking a discount, and hopefully this will work for you. Names have been changed to protect the guilty:

> *Dr. Gimme Discount, M.D.*: Hi Alex, I've got Mrs. Discount on the phone with me here. We just wanted to follow up on our meeting from earlier today. We'd really like to buy that house you showed us, if you think you can get us a deal along the lines we discussed.
>
> *Your Valiant Author*: Thanks Gimme, I am really looking forward to working with you. Would you like me to draft an opening offer today?
>
> *Dr. Gimme Discount, M.D.*: Yes, that would be terrific, but there's just one thing we want to discuss first. We want to buy this house, you see, but we're really pressed for cash. We don't have much of a down payment, and we need to buy furniture and budget for renovations.
>
> *Your Handsome Author*: I understand, and will work on negotiating a financing package that minimizes the down payment required.

Dr. Gimme Discount, M.D.: I know you will, but the thing is we're really low on cash. And, well, there's another agent we've been speaking with and he said he'd rebate 1% of the commission at closing. So, we'd like you to match that, and then you've won our business, you'll be our real estate agent! Okay?

Your Charming Author: Well Gimme, I understand your desire to have a discounted fee. I'd like to let you in on a secret about our industry. Those who discount their fees only do so because they can't get business otherwise. They're probably just starting out in the industry, so they don't have skills or experience, which is not recommended for such an important decision.

Furthermore, you're hiring this person to negotiate on your behalf—if they can't even negotiate their own commission, how good of a job do you think they'll do negotiating for you? So even if we don't work together, I wouldn't recommend that you use the services of someone who discounts.

Dr. Gimme Discount, M.D.: It's just that we're so pressed for cash.

Your Modest Author: I completely understand. I want you to get the best possible outcome, because buying this home is one of the largest financial decisions you will ever make. It's important that whomever you work with can add value to the process, so that they don't cost you anything, and they are putting *more* money in your pocket than their fee.

If you are not 100% convinced that I am capable of bringing that value to the table, then please keep looking until you find that person. Don't go with the discounter, don't go with me, keep looking until you find an expert advisor in whom you have total confidence. This decision is too important to compromise.

FIVE SECONDS OF SILENCE...

Dr. & Mrs. Discount In Unison: No, no, no, no.

Dr. Gimme Discount, M.D.: It's not like that. We want you, we know you're the best. You're our guy. Let's write that offer.

I told them the right thing to do for their own self interest—work with an expert advisor who will add value to this critical transaction. I then let them draw their own conclusion who that person should be.

Since they read my book, they ought to know the value I bring to the table. If the book didn't convince them, then nothing I ever say will convince them either, so why bother? They really are making an important decision, and if they're going to let 1%—one lousy percent!—control the fate of that decision, then they should keep moving until they've found someone who will add at least 1% in value.

The beauty of this conversation is that it turns the lose/lose situation that is most fee conversations into a win/win situation. Either way, I win: either get my full fee, or quickly eliminate a pain in the behind from wasting my valuable time. Remember that money can be replaced, but time cannot. So never undervalue the importance of eliminating time wasters quickly. The prospect also wins: they either get to work with me (I'm awesome!) or they go find someone else who can add more value (ahem, good luck with that).

6 Essential Principals of Maximizing Value and Eliminating Discounts

1. The prospect is making an important decision. They should take it seriously. You take it seriously.

2. If a reduction in fee is driving the decision, the prospect isn't thinking correctly. What matters is return on investment, not the amount of the fee.

3. If the prospect trusts a discounter with their decision, they deserve the results they get—which will be lousy. We don't want them to use a discounter, even if they don't choose us.

4. If you agree to discount, then you deserve the results you get: a pain-in-the-behind client who will make bad decisions and then blame you for them.

5. In virtually any profession, you can make an argument about the self-defeating nature of choosing a discounter. Imagine if you were working with a business coach or consultant who discounted their fees, how could you ever trust their advice? If they themselves aren't capable of getting their full fee, it's foolish to think they can help you get high fees in your business.

   Similarly, lawyers, real estate agents, lenders, contractors and others who negotiate daily in their professions, should never discount. If they can't negotiate their own fees, they certainly can't negotiate well when they represent their clients.

6. You want the prospect to have the best possible outcome with this important decision, and you want them to be confident in

the person who is going to advise them. This is 100% true and don't beat around the bush. Just tell it to them straight.

_____ **is one of the most important decisions you'll ever make; it will impact you and your family for many years to come.**

You should be 100% confident in the value that your advisor brings to the table when you make this critical decision. If you aren't certain that I can put money in your pocket far in excess of my fee, then please, by all means, keep searching for the right person. I want you to get the best outcome for this decision, and if I'm not the right person, please keep searching until you've found an expert advisor in whom you have total confidence.

NOW SHUT UP

The prospect's response will tell you everything you need to know. They either agree or they don't. If they don't and you still take them as a client, then you deserve all the aggravation you are most certainly going to get.

Summary

- When you have literally written the book on the subject, you have tremendous power to protect the integrity of your pricing.

- PI Clients who have read your book will want you, and only you. It would be extremely difficult for a competitor to get the same level of respect in your marketplace.

- Keep your clients' best interests in mind, and stick to your guns on price. They'll make the right decision. If they work with you, that's great. If they don't, they would have been trouble anyway.

WHAT IF I'VE ALREADY STARTED MY BOOK?

Giving up smoking is the easiest thing in the world. I know because I've done it thousands of times.
~ MARK TWAIN, AUTHOR

Even NASA doesn't have the computing power to count the number of unfinished books in the world. Why have so many people started a book and not finished? The chief culprit is taking a completely ad hoc approach. Staring at a blank page is like looking into the abyss.

The wonderful news is that there's a proven process in this book to put you on the fast track to completion. If you already have pages or chapters written, you may be tempted to breeze past steps in the process. Please don't make this mistake!

Invest the time to use the method in your hands. Even if you've written 1,000 pages, please give it a fresh start. You can and will make use of the material you've written—but you may also have to toss some of it overboard. You won't know what to use and what to keep if you haven't embraced the process in earnest.

Please put aside the pages you've written, and start as if you hadn't written any at all. Think of it this way: if you've already wasted months or years on an unfinished book, why not take one more week to use a proven methodology to make massive progress?

Another reason books don't get finished is because people have no accountability. Without a deadline—and a serious consequence if you don't meet that deadline—a project can drag into an unlimited amount of time. **Anyone who spends years on a book and thinks that it's just because the topic is so weighty or important is deluding themselves.** Unless your book requires a year-long medical study, you don't need a year to write a book.

Parkinson's Law brilliantly observes that "work expands so as to fill the time available for its completion." It's as true today as the day it was written, and has been cited by authors from Tim Ferriss to virtually every blogger writing about productivity. It's a very simple rule that is often ignored.

> If you haven't finished your book, you've already got an accountability problem. To make sure you have the best and most current information to help you, there's a free guide available at **GetItDone.PublishToSell.Com**. It contains the most current resources to help you suffer terrible consequences if you fail—er, I mean help you finish your book quickly and cheerfully.

Summary

- Don't let the past dictate your future. Use the methods in this book as if you hadn't written anything before. You can then revisit your unfinished manuscript with a fresh perspective and renewed momentum.

- Don't let the accountability problems you've suffered in the past get the better of you. Use the tools and resources at **GetItDone.PublishToSell.Com** to make sure you stay on track.

- Remember Parkinson's Law: "work expands so as to fill the time available for its completion." Don't give it a lot of time to expand. Crack the whip and get it done yesterday.

THE BCOOL SOLUTION

The first step is you have to say that you can.
~ WILL SMITH, ACTOR

There are five steps to go from zero to done in the *Publish to Sell* way of thinking. These steps will result in a book that delivers PI Clients, and they will get you there in 30 days, if you follow them. Even if there were numerous obstacles and delays beyond your control, you can finish in 60 days. This result is better than 99.999% of people who have ever endeavored to write a book.

Most of the work will be done by other people. Your job is to brainstorm your ideas and either write or speak your manuscript. That can happen in just a week. Once you've given this process your intense focus and have the draft manuscript, there are legions of people who will refine it, polish it and get it into print. You're only working alone for a brief time, and then this becomes a team effort.

The five steps in the BCOOL Solution are:

Brainstorm
Create
Organize
Outsource
Launch

All of these steps are discussed in detail in upcoming chapters. In this chapter, we'll cover the bird's-eye overview. But first, let's talk about what the BCOOL Solution is and is not, so the process makes sense.

What BCOOL Is and What It Can Do for You

- It is a step-by-step process for communicating the value of your expertise and your product or service.
- It is designed with response in mind: elements that will make the reader *need* to reach out to you and get more information—and make it easy for them to do so.
- It is a fast process. You will extract the best ideas and the best knowledge, and get a book out the door quickly.
- It will generate customers long after you've written the book. Those customers will be customers you want, who come to you already indoctrinated in your methods and eager to work with you.
- It will make life very difficult for your competitors. If someone asks a question about a subject, your answer has a great deal more authority when you say, "You are absolutely right, that's a very important question. In fact, I wrote an entire chapter in my book about that very subject." Your competitor is unlikely to be able to respond similarly.

- It will give you a more effective way of introducing yourself. You will be an author—saying that is usually a much more interesting conversation starter than lawyer, accountant, real estate agent, coach, or whatever you may be. Even people you've just met, who couldn't possibly have read your book, will be more inclined to speak to you—and listen.

What BCOOL Is Not

- It's not going to teach you how to be all things to all people. It's about speaking to your best prospects and converting them to PI Clients. It's about talking to people who have the money to afford your services, who will respect your way of doing business, and who can genuinely benefit from your product or service.
- It's not about avoiding offending people and presenting a bland, neutral front. It's about repelling as much as attracting. It's about breaking some eggs to make an omelet.
- It's not ad-hoc writing about what just comes to mind. There is a step-by-step process that extracts the very best ideas in your brain and helps organize them into a book that delivers PI Clients.
- It's not a book that you'll take a year to write. Your book can go from an idea to a paperback sitting in your hands in 30 days. Even with a busy schedule and allowing time for editing, it need not take longer than 60 days. Just follow the process, and the momentum will become unstoppable.
- It's not about telling every last detail of every last step of your product or service. It's educating enough to help people get great results, but not writing an 800-page instruction manual.
- It's not about the latest "shiny object" in marketing. It's about creating a book that will remain valuable for years.

- It's not about holding back important information just to have something to sell later. You should never worry about giving too much information away. Readers who would prefer to do it themselves are customers you don't want. PI Clients will value your service, regardless of how much you have put on paper.

The BCOOL Solution Overview

Below is a brief summary of each step in the BCOOL Solution. A detailed explanation of each step, and how to complete it quickly and painlessly, is contained in the following chapters.

Brainstorm

In this phase, you will extract what you already know and put it on paper. Through a series of questions, you will determine what you want to say in your book. You will think deeply about your industry and your role in it. You'll begin to develop your ideas and outline a schedule for your process. The steps are:

- **Focus on Results**—Establish the outcome required to make this book a success.
- **David vs. Goliath**—Think about your industry, and your place in it, to set the tone for the book and demonstrate your value.
- **Ideal Client**—Describe the client your book will target.
- **Deal Breakers**—Determine which people and behaviors you want to repel.
- **The Good, The Bad, and The Ugly**—Examine the world from the reader's perspective, anticipating their fears, desires, and misconceptions.
- **Fishing with Dynamite**—Learn techniques for understanding your readers so effectively that you'll have an unfair advantage.
- **Offers**—Decide what you will offer your readers in your book to compel them to connect with you.

- **Deadlines**—Outline when are you going to complete each phase of the process?

Create

This is where you become an author. You fashion the raw material from the previous phase into something that has structure and function. In this phase you will either write or speak to create a manuscript. The steps are:

- **Invent a Technology**—Develop intellectual property for your process.
- **Table of Contents**—Write your table of contents. It may only be one page, but a well-done table of contents is make-or-break for the whole manuscript.
- **Offers**—Give free bonuses to the readers that help them, and connect them with you.
- **Manuscript**—Get all of your ideas on the page, in a structure that conforms to the table of contents.
- **Goodies**—Produce the things that you promised in your offer pages.
- **Illustrations**—Begin work on illustrations (if they are needed) as early as possible in the process to avoid holding up the layout.

Organize

Your rough stuff gets spun into gold in this phase. Feedback from editors and readers is used to hone the manuscript into its final form. The steps are:

- **Editing**—Enlist an editor to provide a big-picture review of your book, editing with a meat cleaver instead of a scalpel.
- **Market Feedback**—Listen to what your ideal client has to say about what you've put on the page.

- **Final Manuscript**—Make final edits to ensure that your book is professional and that you've made the copy as punchy and interesting as possible.
- **Chapter Summaries**—Draft chapter summaries from the final manuscript. These summaries help people retain what they've learned, and are simple to create.

Outsource

Your manuscript becomes a book during this phase, with professional artwork and layout. Alternate versions, such as e-books or audiobooks, may also be created. The steps are:

- **Cover**—Create and test your book cover for optimum results.
- **Paperback Layout**—Get a professional layout for your book quickly.
- **Kindle**—Turn the paperback layout into a Kindle electronic book.
- **Audiobooks**—Consider releasing a professionally produced audiobook six months after your book is published.
- **Goodies**—Produce polished versions of your goodies that deliver the value you promised and don't take up a lot of your time.

Launch

This is where your book gets pushed into the world. You'll be strategically giving away copies and integrating the book into your existing marketing. The steps are:

- **Sell in Your Sphere.** Acquire PI Clients and get more business from existing clients and through referrals.

- **Integrate with Existing Marketing**—Use the systems you've already created for your business to maximize the delivery of PI Clients.
- **No List? No Marketing? No Problem**—Start using effective marketing solutions to leverage your time.

Summary

There are 5 steps to the BCOOL Solution that will result in creating your book quickly, and delivering PI Clients for many years to come:

- Brainstorm—Carefully answering very important questions in a structured fashion, to give you the material you need to write your book.

- Create—Writing or speaking your book based upon the work you've done in the Brainstorm phase.

- Organize—Taking the rough diamond of your first manuscript and polishing it into a gem worthy of a crown.

- Outsource—Delegating tasks such as graphic design and layout to specialists who can do great work quickly, and within your budget.

- Launch—Getting your book into to the hands of the right people quickly, so you can get PI Clients without delay or hassle.

BRAINSTORM PART I

Planning Your Book is Like Learning to Survive a Bear Attack

Two men were camping in a remote forest. On a hike they came face to face with a bear. One man drops to the ground, throws off his hiking shoes and slaps on a pair of running shoes. The other man says, "There is no way you can run faster than that bear."

The first man stands up and replies, "I don't have to be faster than the bear. I only have to be faster than you."

~ ANONYMOUS

It is true that writing any book is better than no book, especially when your competition hasn't written a book. And it is true that you only need to run faster than your competition, not faster than the bear.

But...

This thinking has gone too far. Most of the blame falls upon the online marketing "gurus" who peddle pamphlets disguised as books, and the vanity publishers who push books out the door regardless of quality. This has resulted in authors who spend too little time thinking about what goes into their book, and too much time congratulating themselves for the simple fact that there is a book.

It's like training for that bear scenario by making the assumption that there will be someone else who didn't train at all and who is totally out of shape. You are establishing a low bar, and you're setting a lousy tone for dealing with your clients.[2] When you set the bar low, anyone can hop over it. That means you'll generate a lot of semi-committed prospects and half-leads.

We want PI Clients delivered right to us. That is a high bar. Be ready to outrun the bear, even if you'll never have to do so. As you will learn in this book, it's more a matter of knowing what to do than exhaustive effort.

The approach advocated in this book is to raise the bar so that you can survive the bear attack, even if you are alone in the woods. Don't count on lazy competitors; that's not a smart long-term strategy. Just know what to do—and you will by the time you've finished this book—and then do it.

---

[2] Did you know there have been a record number of bear attacks in Florida in recent years? I'm not making this up. Anyway, it turns out that the right thing to do is not to run—and it's not to play dead, as many people falsely believe. As one ranger said, "They eat dead animals all the time, so that's not going to help you."

So what's the right thing to do if you find yourself in the unfortunate situation of being in the presence of an angry Floridian bear? You go flipping crazy on that bear, you shout and scream and wave your arms and make yourself look like you're a zombie on speed.

Or better yet, just avoid places that bears frequent.

So what is the big secret hiding in plain sight? Write a compelling book! Here's the simple formula:

- **Give people a thousand times more value than what they paid for the book.** If your book costs $10 and someone actually applies the information, it should be worth $10,000 to them at the very least. Indeed, if people apply what they've learned numerous times over their lifetime, the return should be astronomical.
- **Don't be afraid to reveal too much information.** The best prospects will value what you've given them, and be eager to pay for greater service and greater results—no matter how much information you reveal. On the other hand, the people who want to do it themselves will never become PI Clients, and are therefore not worth worrying about.
- **Don't be afraid to offend people or make people angry.** Speak your truth, as you know it and live it, and attract the people who are like-minded. Repel the people that don't get it. It's much better to have the people you don't want remove themselves from your world before you waste time with them. Your book can keep them away, like garlic repelling vampires.

Everything should be made as simple as possible, but no simpler.
~ ALBERT EINSTEIN, NOBEL PRIZE WINNING PHYSICIST

The method in *Publish To Sell* is designed to make authoring as simple as possible—and still produce a professional book of enduring value. You could produce a book in a day, but that's not going to deliver PI Clients for many years. Alternatively, some people take years to write a book, and that book is no more effective from the extra time. *Publish to Sell* is not too fast and not too slow. It's just right for our objective: delivering PI Clients quickly.

Summary

- Your book is designed to get you PI Clients, not leads or prospects. Leads and prospects will happen, but don't confuse a side-effect with the goal.

- Give the reader a thousand times more value than what they paid for your book.

- Be generous with your readers, give away your secrets. The people who will become PI Clients will trust you more for your generosity, and the do-it-yourself crowd wasn't going to become PI Clients anyway.

- It's okay to offend and repel people. You don't want every person for a client, and you may as well weed out people who aren't compatible with you right away.

BRAINSTORM PART II

Step by Step

To get through an impossible situation, you don't need the reflexes of a Grand Prix driver, the muscles of a Hercules, the mind of an Einstein. You simply need to know what to do.
~ ANTHONY GREENBACK, THE BOOK OF SURVIVAL

The *Brainstorming* part of the BCOOL Solution is the secret sauce. When you think through the process in this structured fashion, it makes writing much easier. Without this method, you get the typical frustrations and the "I've been working on my book for a year" non-result of most authors.

In the brainstorming phase, you will begin implementing the techniques and approaches explained earlier in this book. This is a fun phase, because you get to play like a child. Like every game, there are rules. So this creative play is structured to be effective, and will result in quickly producing a superb blueprint for your book.

The blueprint you will have at the end of this process will clarify the value that you provide, and the process by which you provide it. You'll have clear and straightforward answers to important questions, which will dramatically improve your manuscript. If you ever get stumped by any question, just jot down (or speak and record) the best answer that comes to mind. A poor answer is better than no answer at all. It's still a step forward.

The eight things you will want to think about before you even start writing your book are outlined in the steps below. **Please don't skip any of the steps. If you do, the writing process will be a lot more time-consuming and frustrating.** I'm giving you the secret sauce here. Please use it!

Focus on Results

Before we proceed with any project, we should have a clear sense of why we are doing it in the first place. In this case, we already know the purpose of your book is to deliver PI Clients for many years to come.

However, let's take that a step further and quantify it. What is the minimum result you need to make this process worth your time? We will of course hope and expect to beat that, but let's set the bar. What kind of return on investment makes this process worthwhile for you?

To answer that, you'll have to know something about the lifetime value of a PI Client. PI Clients will do business with you for years. Your book will keep delivering PI Clients for many years, too. Thus, over the long term, it's pretty tough to imagine you will not get a stellar return on the time and money you invest in your book. A lifetime may be too long to consider, so let's value our clients over ten years. That way, if every human being stops reading books in eleven years, we still made money!

> **Based on the ten-year value of your PI Clients, how many clients need to be delivered in the first year to make this worth your effort?**
>
> Here is an example. Let's assume the average luxury home sale is worth $45,000 in commissions. Within ten years, I'd expect a PI Client to do an average of at least two transactions. Let's also imagine that 25% of clients refer another PI Client within ten years. All of these are very conservative assumptions, but since we're making a long-term projection, it's better to be conservative than aggressive.
>
> So, one PI Client's ten-year value is
>
> > 2 transactions + .25 referral transaction = 2.25 transactions
> > * $45,000 per transaction
> > = $101,250 total revenue
>
> Thus, one PI Client is quite a good return on the time and money it took to create the book. Just one client!

Of course one would expect to get many more clients as a result of the book. Let's imagine you stopped promoting the book after the first few months. You will still get clients because (1) books sit on people's desks, shelves, tablets and smartphones and serve as a long-term reminder of your products or services; and (2) some people will find them on Amazon and other bookstores without your promotion.

Thus, it seems highly implausible to get less than five PI Clients over time, even if you weren't aggressively promoting your book. Using the math above, just five clients would be worth more than $500,000 to a luxury real estate agent in a middle-priced U.S. market.

Personally, I find these numbers more than compelling. Alas, maybe you eat gold-plated corn flakes for breakfast and you need a bigger return to make it worth your while. Whatever your financial situation, come up with a value for your PI Clients, and determine how many you'll need to make this project a success.

It is entirely reasonable to get 50, 100, or more PI Clients over the lifetime of your book. I deliberately chose very small numbers above to show you that a book done using the *Publish to Sell* method is worth your time—even with the most conservative assumptions. You just need to offer a high value product or service, and if you do, the math really is a no-brainer.

Once you have your specific numbers in front of you, it ought to be sufficient motivation to keep you moving. If your numbers aren't compelling, you may not be charging enough for your product or service. Your book is a fantastic tool to enable you to raise prices. If you provide great value, start actually getting paid for it.

David vs. Goliath

Your industry is Goliath. You are David, the underdog about to take it down. You'll have to make your reader understand what Goliath is about, why he is ripe to go down, why your way is better, and what value you bring to the table. To that end, take a few minutes to answer the following questions now, and write down your answers:

- What are the most important, widespread problems in your industry?
- Why will so few people in the industry admit to these problems?

- What profit motives does the industry have for keeping the status quo?
- When is the client not "always right?"
- What goes wrong for clients when they buy solely based on price?
- What does David do differently that that makes him the champion for his clients?

The answers to these questions will be critical throughout the writing and editing process. These answers are also effective tools to break through writer's block. When I think about the nonsense in my industry, it makes me angry—it's very easy to come up with stuff to say when I'm ticked off. Just channel your anger and frustration toward a positive outcome, a change, or an alternative—and you have something valuable.

Ideal Client

There's a temptation to talk about clients like children: "Oh, I love them all equally," but the fact is all clients are *not* created equally. Think of the best client you've ever had, a situation where you made a great deal of money, and you really enjoyed working with them. At the time you probably thought, "if only they could all be like this." Well, you *can* work with superb clients all the time, and publishing your book will make it easy.

Your best client ever is the target for your book. We're not going to be vague and do some "dream client" exercise like you may have seen in other marketing books or courses. Instead, let's pick a real person to make the goal very clear. You know this person. You know what's important to them, what they dislike, and, most importantly, how they do business. Post a photo or their name somewhere where you will see it every day you write. Your best client is now your muse.

The fact of the matter is that the best client you've worked with in real life is a client you can work with again. If all your clients were like your best client, wouldn't you be thrilled? Our job is to multiply that best client. Even if you've only found someone of that quality once before, in the future you should have many.

Write down answers to the following questions:

- Who is the best client you've ever had? Be specific, just one person. If you sell to large corporations, focus on the primary decision maker at the company.
- What made them a great customer for you?
- What were their characteristics—age, marital status, home town, kids, favorite food and drink, hobbies?
- What are their favorite books and what have they read recently? If you don't know, it's a great time to reconnect for a friendly chat.
- How did they find you? If by referral, from whom? If through your marketing, which campaign?
- What do you think would be the most irresistible subject for a book for them, a book that they would HAVE to grab off the shelf? Imagine as if you are writing a book just for that one person.
- How did they conduct their business differently than most clients?
- What questions did they ask before making a decision to buy from you?
- What other interesting or unusual characteristics define this person?

In all of the above, pay careful attention to the things that the best client did that most clients do not do, and vice versa. If you've had a handful of dream clients, feel free to repeat this exercise to determine their common characteristics. But if your third-best customer was only worth half as much as your best, just stick with #1—unless that most valuable client was a jerk. Quality is way, way more important than quantity.

Deal Breakers
What is the stuff that you have put up with begrudgingly that you never want to experience again? Here are some examples of things that I dealt with from bad clients that I would never tolerate again:

- They want access to me at any time, not just during my working hours.
- They refuse to make decisions, and we waste countless hours with nonsensical pondering and emotional roller coaster riding.
- They want me to discount my fees.

You may have encountered similar problems. Whatever they may be, list them all. We are going to banish them in the book, educating people never to do those things if they wish to work with you. This is detoxifying the poisons of past bad clients and inoculating ourselves against new ones with Vitamin B—boundaries.

- What customers do you not want? Think of the worst you've encountered.
- What traits do the worst customers have in common?
- How did they find you? If by referral, from whom? If through your marketing, which campaign?
- What do you think would be the most irresistible subject for a book for them? Have fun with it. For example: "The Indecisive Cheapskate's Guide to Hiring a Lawyer for a Critically Important Business Contract."

- When and how will you be accessible to clients?
- What are your pet peeves? Get it all on the page—exorcise those demons!

Your book is a fantastic tool to erect 12-foot-tall, iron-clad boundaries that stop unacceptable behavior before it gets started—without having any uncomfortable conversations.

The Good, The Bad, and The Ugly

Now that we have thought deeply about our industry and our own business, we are ready to dive into the most important perspective: the perspective of the reader. Specifically, we want to define the terrible life the reader will have when they make the wrong decision, and we want to describe the glorious life that awaits them when they make the right decision. We also want to describe some of the common misconceptions readers are likely to have—the ugly truth.

Please don't censor yourself. Put all your thoughts on paper, no matter how insignificant or silly an idea may seem.

The Good

The reader has something in mind when they open this book, something they want. We want to think more deeply about what that may be.

- If you could wave a magic wand and give the reader anything, what would they ask you for? Don't limit yourself to what you can deliver. Think of the client's dream scenario.
- How will the reader's life change if they follow your instructions? Don't settle for a small answer. It has to be something that passes the pillow talk test.

- What does it do that they would want to tell their spouse gleefully? Does it give them more freedom? Does it make them happier? Write down as many things as come to mind.

The Bad

Assuming they haven't had access to the brilliant techniques in your book nor your services, the readers are not happy campers. Let's stir the pot, twist the knife, shake up the bag. Do not let them off the hook, tell them what's happening now and why it sucks.

- What do we know must be a problem for them simply by virtue of the fact that they are reading your book? For example, if your book is about online marketing, then clearly the reader wants more customers.
- What problems have the readers likely experienced related to your service or product? Someone seeking online marketing help may have previously wasted a lot of money on advertising or consulting.
- How does this impact their business, and their life? It's critical to bring this home. "Not getting enough sales" is not nearly as scary as "not knowing how I'm going to pay the mortgage for my family's home." Let's understand and articulate the reader's real problem.

The Ugly

Sometimes, what we say we want isn't really what we want. Other times, what we want isn't really what's best for us. Based on your experience in your industry, record some of the more common misconceptions and mistakes that clients and customers have made and are likely to make.

- Is their wish the core desire or a substitute? For example, if a prospective client says, "I want my website to rank #1 on Google," what they really mean is, "I want more business." After all, nobody cares about search engine rankings for their own sake, it's a means to an end. When you dig deeper, what the prospect would probably say is that they want more revenue. Dig deeper still, and it's actually more income. Dig even further, and it's more freedom to spend time with family.
- What does the reader *think* they want that is misguided? In every industry, people often express a desire for X, when in fact Y is better or more relevant. In your experience, what are the common scenarios in which a client starts off thinking they need X but they really need Y? Your book is a great opportunity to move them to the correct path.
- What is the most counterintuitive thing you have learned about your clients? In other words, what did you absolutely expect to be true that has turned out in so many cases to be false?

Fishing with Dynamite

Warning! This technique is very powerful, and will transform your knowledge of your readers and your market. That's a great thing, of course. However, it is important that you have answered the questions in the preceding sections before you use these techniques. Your book is a personal statement, and you want to have your own thoughts on paper before you start flooding your brain—and your writing—with the powerful knowledge of your readers you will learn with these techniques.

Have you answered the questions in the preceding sections? If so, please read on…

While we don't care about writing a bestseller, there is a very powerful technique that takes advantage of bestselling books in order to understand what is going on in the mind of readers. Imagine, if you will, the ability to know the very sentences that are most important to readers, to know down to the word what people in your audience find most interesting and compelling. Amazingly enough, Amazon delivers this information—for free—thanks to the magic of Kindle.

Specifically, you can see the Popular Highlights, culled from every book on Kindle. At present, it is way, way down at the bottom of the sales page, and you typically have to scroll the equivalent of three screens down to see it. It's worth digging for the treasure trove of insights you can gather from Popular Highlights.

Here are some of the types of books for which you should be doing this valuable research:

- **Current and all-time bestsellers in your category.** We must, after all, get into the mind of Goliath if we are going to take him down.
- **Books from authors that have a similar audience to the one you'd like to have.** For example, if you wanted to write a book about sales and you envy the audience of Zig Ziglar, then read the popular highlights from his books.
- **Related purchases to the books above.** For every book sold on Amazon there's a list of "other items customers bought after viewing this item." You may discover related authors you did not know. Find out what passages in those books are resonating with readers, because clearly the audiences overlap.
- **Books from popular authors that you think are dead wrong.** Perhaps you are writing a sales book and you think Zig Ziglar's way of thinking is outdated. You may be right, but clearly there

are a lot of readers who disagree. Before you throw the baby out with the bathwater, learn what passages resonate the most with his readers. Maybe ole Zig ain't all bad. Or maybe he really is that bad, and you'll have some great material to rant against in your book.

This extraordinary free resource is like having x-ray vision. You can see through all the bluster and the hype, and learn what's really going on in the mind of the reader. Whether you agree with what you find in these books or not, in just an hour or two you will gain powerful insight.

Copy and paste any interesting quotes into a document, then refer back to them to spur you along in your writing process. Be sure not to limit yourself to quotes where you agree. Those you think are complete nonsense can be equally helpful to your writing.

Offers

Plan to create at least two offers to make available to your readers. I'd recommend planning several, because as you proceed you may decide that some aren't up to snuff. Alternatively, you may realize you are onto something extremely valuable that may become its own product. In either case, if you start with five ideas, you may wind up with only two or three offers for the book.

Please see the following chapter for greater detail on the critical matter of creating offers. For now, just jot down any ideas you may have.

Deadlines

Thrive on deadlines, nothing brings on inspiration more readily than desperation.
~ Harry Shearer, actor

DON'T MESS AROUND WITH DEADLINES. SET THEM AND ARRANGE YOUR WORLD TO MAKE SURE YOU HIT THEM.

Why be so tough? A week becomes a month becomes a year becomes a someday. Push yourself, it's worth it. It's only a workweek to do the manuscript, or less. From there, you can give yourself a week to get through each of the other phases—which will mostly be done by other people, so your time burden will drop dramatically after the first week.

Set the deadline, and take it seriously. I recommend targeting 30 days to launch, which means one week for the manuscript and three weeks for all the rest. If you are speaking your book and working with a ghostwriter, it may take a month to get a finished manuscript instead of a week. From there, the process works on the same schedule. Under virtually no circumstances should you budget more than 60 days.

No matter what you choose, make sure it's *uncomfortable*. If you are projecting a leisurely pace, you've already given up before you started. You should have to hustle to get this done. Hustle is good, there's money in hustle. It's just a short sprint, then you can go back to your normal schedule. When you get done with this sprint, you'll be earning more and working with more enjoyable clients for many years to come.

The only phase in this process that can be a valid reason to delay is feedback from your best clients and prospects. Their comments are hugely valuable to the editing process. It can be challenging to give people a deadline when they're doing you a favor. Bribe them however you can to get a reasonably quick response. Alternatively, just give people a chapter or two to get them started, and then if they get excited, they'll be more likely to breeze through the rest.

If you give people only one chapter to read, make it your first chapter. After all, the first chapter's sole job is to make the reader want to read the next chapter. If it accomplishes the mission, and they are asking you for more, you're in great shape. If you hear crickets after they read the first chapter, ask your editor to pay special attention to it.

> Nothing in this book will work if you don't apply it. Most books are never finished, let alone published, because people aren't accountable. To make sure you finish what you start, visit **GetItDone.PublishToSell.Com**. You will find the most current resources to help you finish what you start, and it's free.

Summary

- The structured brainstorming process is the "secret sauce" of *Publish to Sell*. The disappointment experienced by most business book authors comes from a lack of this structured thinking process. **If you only take action on one chapter in this whole book, please make it this one.**

- Knowing the value of your PI Clients is absolutely critical to every step of your book. Most people never run the numbers, and without those numbers, it's easy to lose motivation. It's also impossible to market your book effectively. So, please be sure to do the exercise in the Focus On Results section.

- Thinking deeply about your ideal client, your industry, and the value you provide is important for your book. It will also impact your business strategy and your relationships with clients, employees, and vendors. It's impossible to overstate the importance of these exercises. Most of my clients rave about what they learn and how it improves their business—before they've even started the first page of their manuscript.

BRAINSTORM PART III

The Most Important Page in Your Book

Sell something. America needs the business.
~ Zig Ziglar, author

Authoring and publishing a book is a failure unless it delivers PI Clients. What type of clients? *PI Clients—Profitable Implementors.* Specifically:

- Clients who are fun. Life is too short to deal with people who have no sense of humor.
- Clients who value your advice and implement what you tell them to do.
- Clients who work on your terms and respect your boundaries.
- Clients who have a track record of success, and are thus likely to be successful getting results with your product or service.

In order to get PI Clients, you must have <u>one critical page in your book</u>: the offer. If you don't make the reader an offer, if you don't provide a way for them to reach out to you, then this is all for naught.

Sales is a process. Your book goes a long way to move the right people far along the path to becoming a PI Client. However, the book is not the whole process. The offer acts as a bridge to connect them with you and to make it easy for readers to take advantage of your valuable products or services. You must have a compelling offer in your book, and preferably several.

The offers you put in your book depend on your existing marketing process, and the type of product or service you sell. So, whether you are using video, a Facebook group, direct mail, or something else, you are going to want to leverage these existing skills and resources.

If you don't have a marketing process that's automated, then email is a no brainer. You set it up once, and you can continue to use it for years, updating or expanding only as needed. If you already have a landing page and email system but it's giving you headaches, rest assured there are easy and effective tools available. To learn the most current recommendations for quick and easy landing pages and email, visit **Recommendations.PublishToSell.Com**. Well goodness gracious, I just made you an offer—see how easy that was?

Sprinkle your book with offers. Here are some characteristics of successful offers:

- **Valuable**—Provide something of real value to the reader. Don't shill for the sake of email addresses or tweets or Facebook followers. Give readers something that they can use and that is congruent with our value proposition: delivering something worth at least 1,000 times the cost of the book.

- **Systematic**—Whatever you offer should be easily automated or outsourced. Don't offer a consultation or something that requires your time. Provide something that has evergreen value, and that requires the same amount of effort whether 10 people or 10,000 want it.

- **Timely, but Stands the Test of Time**—Remember that this book is a ten-year plan, and you want the book you publish to stand on its own in ten years. We all have enough marketing methods that require constant "care and feeding," Your book is meant to be a steady, consistent creator of clients without continuous effort. Thus, you should remove the content that's likely to become stale in a year, and make that into one of the goodies you will offer as a bonus.

What you offer should complement and enhance the book after ten years—even if that means updating it occasionally. Don't create something that only has value for a month; the only exception would be if you are already doing something like this in your marketing and have processes in place to handle the work. The book is meant to make your life easier and deliver PI Clients, so keep it simple.

- **Leverage Existing Marketing**—Perhaps you have an email newsletter or a direct mail newsletter that is an important part of your marketing process. Or maybe you have a Facebook group that's very active. Something that's already humming and has proven itself to have value is certainly a great offer for your book.

However, don't direct people who have read the book and want to be high-value PI Clients to some old marketing process that you may have built when you were selling lower-value products. If your other marketing isn't congruent with the PI Client you are targeting in the book, then don't include it as an offer.

- **Different Modality from Your High-Value Product or Service**—If your service is delivered via phone, then you certainly don't want to be giving away a free sample phone consultation. That totally devalues your service, and rightly, people will resist paying for what they got for free. So, for example, if you deliver via phone, then your valuable free offers should be on paper. If you charge for a Facebook mastermind, then don't create a free mastermind. Instead, give people some video.

Whatever you do, keep your free offers in a different medium or modality than the higher-value service. The only exception would be if you already have a proven sales technique, e.g. using video to sell a video course. Otherwise, it's best to keep these channels separate.

In most businesses, this will be easy. For example, a financial advisor is typically doing his/her highest value work face to face. But in some businesses, there could be a temptation to give away the golden goose. Don't do it. Deliver real value in your book and your free offers, but make sure that your best clients are getting the most value, and that it's not being diluted.

The Four Most Common Types of Readers

When you are crafting your offer—and throughout the writing and publishing of your book—it's helpful to keep in mind the four most common reactions of your readers.

1. **Gotta Have It**—Bullseye! There's a meeting of the minds. These readers want to work with you however possible, and at any cost that will deliver them return on investment. These are the people we should have at the top of our minds throughout the whole process.

2. **Want It, "Can't" Afford It**—There is a meeting of the minds here, too, but the these readers don't have sufficient resources to make use of your high-value services... yet. Or, more probably, they have the resources, but aren't fully committed to using them. For example, they "can't" find $10,000 to grow their business or get fit or (substitute your service here)—and yet, if they were to find themselves in jail, $10,000 of bail money would materialize very quickly. They've got it, they just don't want to use it. Yet.

   The folks in this category are your future clients, the ones that you can cultivate over the long term. If you start building a relationship with them now, they will be totally indoctrinated to your way of working by the time they make the leap to your level.

   There are some very high value services that I've bought, but I lingered and looked for a long time before I made the plunge. If you've ever bought a very high-end product or service, you probably have done the same. So keep these folks in mind, because they are your second priority. They are your long-term bread and butter.

3. **DIY 'til I Die**—The motto of these readers is Do It Yourself (DIY) in all things, regardless of how badly they do it, or how much time they waste. These people do not understand the concept of return on investment. Their whole lives revolve around clipping coupons and never letting a dollar leave their wallet. When they do hire someone, they always pick the low bid. There's an old saying, "the most expensive contractor you'll ever hire is the one who gives you the lowest bid." Evidently, these folks haven't heard it enough times to believe it.

You should wish them well—from a healthy distance. Don't try to convert them. Don't expend your energy speaking to them. They need a "spiritual conversion" before they will move into one of the first two categories. Unless spiritual conversion is your business model, forget them.

4. **Haters**—These are the folks who let you know you're doing your job. If there are no haters, you have failed to craft a message that takes a strong position. If you haven't taken a strong position, then what kind of expert are you?

In a sense, haters are actually more valuable than the DIY folks. You should pay attention to haters, because they can unintentionally produce great marketing opportunities and interesting ideas. There's nothing more satisfying than getting a great marketing opportunity from the enemy. ☺

So with all that in mind, begin to craft an offer. Here are some examples:

- **Recommendations**—Lists of vendors, services, blogs, or whatever else you recommend. Since your recommendations will likely change over time, it's especially appropriate to use these for a bonus instead of putting them in the book.
- **Templates**—Specific tasks that they can accomplish by modeling or using your template. This could be an Excel spreadsheet, an email they can copy, or whatever else is relevant.
- **Video**—You can record a video to elaborate on a subject or to bond with your audience and showcase your personality.
- **Audio**—Record your book as an audiobook and give it away to readers. Or you can record some podcasts. There are lots of possibilities, and this can be a good option for people who aren't comfortable with video.
- **Action Guide**—Create a step-by-step guide and/or checklist that your readers can use to implement what you've taught them.
- **Webinar**—Answer reader questions in a webinar or present a topic of interest. Once you have completed it, you can use replays as evergreen content.

To get a more detailed understanding of great offers, it helps to have a "swipe file" of offers from other companies. You can then refer to them for inspiration. Pay careful attention to what other successful marketers are doing, and the types of offers they are making. Do not limit yourself to your own industry, make an effort to look at others. If you stick with just your own industry, you may be repeating messages that your prospects have already heard.

Summary

- No offer, no money—it's as simple as that. If you want your book to *do* something instead of just sitting on a shelf, then creating powerful offers is critical.

- We are trying to deliver value equal to 1,000 times the cost of the book, and the resources you offer are part of that. Don't cut corners, create materials of real value. Sell to your reader the way you would want to be sold yourself.

- There is no need to be pushy with offers. Your offers should be genuinely valuable to the reader, and sell themselves. Just do a good job of explaining what's available, and inserting them in relevant sections of your book.

- When crafting your offers, keep in mind that you are working to attract PI Clients. You don't have to provide every bit of minutiae to satisfy the urges of a do-it-yourselfer, who will never be a fit for your business. Add value, but remember who you are trying to serve.

BRAINSTORM PART IV

Attention Ikea Shoppers

A goal without a plan is just a wish.
~ Antoine de Saint-Exupéry, author

You are writing a book about a topic you already know well. You have lived it, you have experience, and you have a lot of knowledge. However, getting that information out of your brain and onto the page is daunting without a step-by-step plan. That's why most people have never even tried to author a book, and most of those that do try never finish.

If you start a book without a step-by-step plan, it's like you've bought a living room set at Ikea with no instructions. You just have a giant pile of parts sitting on your floor. You don't know which parts are for which pieces of furniture. You don't know how the parts fit together. You don't even know for certain whether you have the right parts, some duplicates or if you are missing parts altogether.

The amount of aggravation and effort involved in putting together the furniture would be a hundred times greater without the instruction manual. You may start putting things together randomly, thinking that you are making progress only to learn you have made a critical mistake and have to disassemble something.

You would almost certainly be quite a miserable person to be around, shouting words unsuitable for children to hear, and unattractive to your significant other. In the end, you'd probably decide it was a stupid project, clear out the living room and try to forget it ever happened.

This simple metaphor explains why so many people fail when writing a book. They believe the information is in their brain, which is absolutely true. However, they completely underestimate the importance of a proven step-by-step process. They buy the furniture without the instruction manual, virtually guaranteeing an unpleasant experience leading to disappointment and failure.

Publish to Sell is like the instruction manual for Ikea furniture. You already own the parts, and by applying what you learn in this book, you will finish what you start. You'll get the results you expect, without the trouble, delay, or cost of an ad hoc process.

It's important to note that Ikea furniture isn't perfect—and we don't expect the book to be perfect. Like Ikea furniture, your book is a compromise. When we get something that we like 80% as much as a piece that costs 25 times more, then we are okay with the compromise. In a similar vein, don't expect your book to be perfect. It will never be perfect, and indeed there is no perfect piece of furniture—or book—no matter how much money or time we spend. PI Clients are our goal, not perfection.

Personally, I stopped assembling furniture from Ikea years ago. The first time I paid someone to assemble furniture for me, it was a revelation. It was like the first time I paid movers to pack my stuff. I saw the amazing efficiency they brought and said to myself, "Never, ever, ever again will I do this myself." Experts who do something day in and day out are so much better than novices who do it occasionally. The results are dramatically better, they finish in a fraction of the time, and they work far more elegantly.

If you are like-minded and prefer not to go it alone, there may be some help available at **Help.PublishToSell.Com**. You'll have assistance to break through obstacles and answer questions. You'll have an experienced sounding board to listen to ideas and help you refine them. While I do greatly enjoy helping people, there are only so many projects in which I can be directly involved. Thus, if you have an interest, please visit the site sooner rather than later, as there may be a wait before help becomes available.

Regardless of whether you get help or proceed on your own, the most important thing is to take action. If you're going to do it yourself, then please get started on the Brainstorming part of the BCOOL solution *now* if you haven't already. If you're going to get help, then please request it *now*. If you close this book and "think about it" before taking action, the odds of failure go up dramatically.

There isn't any reason to read the next chapter until you've finished the exercises in the Brainstorming section. Please take action immediately, start laying the foundation that will make you successful and separate yourself from the millions of people who are thinking about authoring a book someday.

Summary

- What separates you from 99.999% of all authors is that you have a plan. The plan will make the process easier and the results better.

- You can and will succeed as long as you take action.

- Don't even turn the page. Get to work on the exercises in the Brainstorming section immediately. Please ☺

CREATE PART I

Writing by the Pound

Move fast, break stuff.
~ Mark Zuckerberg, Co-founder of Facebook

The most common mistake people make when they hear that we need to create a high quality book is they assume that it will take a long time. While there are many things in life where there's a tradeoff between speed and quality, this is not always true in writing. More specifically, it's not true in the writing process for a book to deliver PI Clients.

You *can* produce a lot of writing quickly, and have it be very effective. In fact, there is a strong argument to be made that writing too slowly produces a book of lower quality.

The goal is to get your important ideas out there in a way that people can understand them. If you spend too long staring at that page, your cognitive ability is diminished. You are pedaling harder but not going anywhere. Then, when you spend a lot of time and have little to show for it, your motivation becomes sapped. It's a vicious cycle.

Create a virtuous circle of writing by getting it done quickly. Once you see that you have the makings of a real book in front of you, it will motivate you, and you'll see it through. Don't worry about the quality. Quality will be addressed during editing, but you can't get to editing until you have a manuscript.

Get over any perfectionist tendencies, and put some words on paper. Put a *lot* of words on paper. Speed and momentum are so much more important than quality at this stage. One bad sentence doesn't destroy a paragraph, and one bad chapter doesn't destroy a book. Indeed ten bad chapters don't necessarily destroy a book—editors exist for a reason.

No matter how great a writer may be, they still need an editor. Whatever you write is going to be rewritten and revised. Therefore, **don't try to play editor at the same time that you write, just get the ideas out there in some form or fashion.**

You should weigh the words by the pound! Don't judge them by how clever they are, but by their quantity. Get it all out there—all of it—on the page. Quickly. The sooner you do that, the sooner an editor (or two or three) can polish your words into fine gems. But without the raw material, the process stops.

What if you've never written? What if you can't type? What if? What if? What if?

No problem! If you have such a terrible fear of writing that you can't even sit at the keyboard, don't worry. Just speak into the microphone, let someone else transcribe it, and pay a writer to turn your spoken words into a coherent structure. Four recorded hours of speaking on your subject should provide plenty of material for a book, even after throwing out the garbage.

If you find it difficult to speak at length on the subject on your own, record yourself speaking with a client—or pay a journalist to interview you. Also, you can do this sixty minutes at a time, so you don't get worn out. You don't need to sit for four hours straight. You don't even need to do all the interviews with the same person.

You'll have to pay more to create your book by recording it, but it *will* get done. Just because someone edits the order and selects what to put in the final document doesn't mean you aren't the author. These are *your* ideas and *your* words, they're just edited. Some people's writing will require more editing and some will require less, but it's editing all the same.

People who record their books will require help from outsourcers. So, in addition to editors, people who record will want to find help with transcription and ghostwriting early in the process. For current techniques and resources, please visit **NoWriting.PublishToSell.Com**.

> *The deadline is the greatest invention in the history of the world. Without it, nothing else would have been invented.*
> ~ **JOHN CARLTON**, COPYWRITER

Regardless of whether you write or speak your book, finish your book in one week. If you are speaking, you really have no excuse to take longer than a few days. If you are writing, then you should look at your calendar and block out time. Block out 40 hours—one workweek. So, if you can only budget 10 hours per week, then your work is spread over four weeks. You may not need this much time, but better to schedule it anyway. You'll be amazed at how quickly you can write after you've answered the questions and structured your thinking.

Whatever you do, make the commitment. Don't spend 3 hours watching TV, spend that time writing until you are finished. You'll get it done before you know it, and your life will change as a result of the work you've done. Television will not change your life, nor will any other distractions. If you're having trouble with accountability, then please visit **GetItDone.PublishToSell.Com** for free resources to keep you on track.

You don't need to finish the perfect book, you just want enough on paper so that the professionals you hire have something to work with. If you try to write for a couple of days and aren't getting quick results, then speak the book. Or if you come out of the gate strong and then lose inspiration after a couple of days, switch to speaking.

Without the initial push of the deadline and the resulting momentum in that first week, your book will likely end up another entry on the long list of "things I'm going to do someday." When you have a completed manuscript, you have given birth to your project. It grows from that point on, it has its own energy, and people are drawn to it.

Here's another metaphor that may help explain the need for speed: in order for a rocket ship to break through the Earth's atmosphere, it has to expend a huge amount of energy very quickly to attain launch velocity. Once it has passed the Earth's atmosphere, the rocket will continue its trajectory for many years with a tiny fraction of the fuel initially required.

Commit to getting all of the material of your book into a manuscript in one week, and it becomes a reality. The rest of the steps—the editing and production—are easy by comparison. They feel inevitable once the manuscript is done.

It seems like all the other steps in the process are preordained once the manuscript is complete. Before that point, the whole project is a maybe. It's an idea. It's ephemeral. If you fail to make this commitment to one week, you will be "working on a book" a year from now.

Speed will reward you in so many ways. Your writing will be clear because you won't have time to think about complicated ways to say things. Once it's a manuscript it's no longer just an idea, it is real. From that point on, the wind is at your back, and professionals will be helping you cross the finish line.

Speed is essential to quality and to progress. Commit to a one week deadline. If you write two chapters a day for seven days, or record four to five hours of dialogue in total, you are there.

Your manuscript doesn't need to be perfect, or even close to it. It just needs to exist.

Summary

- Speed will reward you in many ways. Your writing will be clear because you won't have time to think about complicated ways to say things.

- You don't need to write a book to be an author. If you want to speak your book, the most current tools and resources are at **NoWriting.PublishToSell.Com**.

- Commit to getting all of the material for your book into a manuscript in one week, and it becomes a reality. The rest of the steps—the editing and production—are easy by comparison. They feel inevitable once the manuscript is done.

- One week can be divided up however you wish. For me, carving out some time in one calendar week (and allowing a lot of the other balls I'm juggling in life to drop) works well. For you, maybe four hours a day on weekends is better. Just make a plan, and if you are worried about accountability, look at some of the tools and resources available at **GetItDone.PublishToSell.Com**.

CREATE PART II

Step by Step

How do you eat an elephant?
One bite at a time.
~ ANONYMOUS

Writing a book is a scary prospect in most people's minds. It's painful if you don't have a method, because it's like your brain has to fight the emptiness of the universe to pull something out of the ether. You won't be doing that here. We have a much easier way.

The BCOOL Solution is like building with Legos: it's simple. Most of the time, you build something that works and is fun, and it doesn't take a long time to do it. Sometimes you build something that sucks, but it's pretty easy to just reassemble the pieces into something better. You've done the preliminary work. You've answered the questions in the Brainstorming chapters, and now you're ready to take action and start creating your content.

Become an Inventor

In this phase, you will be organizing your magic into a process that you name, so that it belongs to you, is associated with you, and makes it easy for people to learn. The next chapter explains this in great detail. You may call it a process, a solution, a method—whatever resonates with you. The important thing is to have a clear, step-by-step recipe that gets results for the reader.

Table of Contents

Creating a well-organized table of contents is absolutely critical. Even if you are going to dictate your entire book, or get it ghostwritten based on interviews, you still need a table of contents. Without a strong table of contents, your writing (or speaking, as it were) will go off the rails quickly. You'll have thousands of disconnected words you can't organize, and it's a completely avoidable problem.

Offers

Write the "sales pages" for your offers. List the benefits and use punchy copy to get people excited. It's helpful to know what you're going to use as a bridge to the next step of your relationship with clients before you complete the manuscript. Of course, if you get stuck here or are unhappy with what you wrote, you can hire an editor or copywriter to help.

Manuscript

Some people freak out at the idea of writing a book. They imagine themselves battling a blank page searching for inspiration. But it's not nearly as big a deal as many people think. Writing only becomes a big deal when you leave the project open-ended and let it take up an obscene amount of time.

The most important things to remember are:

1. **You don't need to write a perfect book**, and you don't even need to write a good book—there are a million people with master's degrees dying to fix even the most messed up manuscript.
2. **Commit to completing it in one workweek**—no excuses. Put the time on your calendar, and make sacrifices when necessary to get it done. You only have to do this for a short time, and you will benefit for many years. It's worth the hustle.
3. **Write like you were going to weigh your words by the pound**, and pay no attention to quality in this phase.
4. **A bad manuscript written in one week is way more profitable than an awesome manuscript that takes two years.** Both are going to get edited, and it's the edited version that matters, not the first draft.

I don't advocate any special tool for writing except to go with what you already know. For example, I started writing this book with an application called WriteRoom. It was designed to be very low tech and keep me focused on the writing. It doesn't even offer simple formatting like bold and italics; it's strictly about getting words on the page. Once I had a critical mass of words and wanted something more sophisticated, I used Microsoft Word. However, you can use a text editor, pen and paper, or whatever else may be comfortable. Don't mess around with technology, just get your words out there.

If you prefer to speak, that's fine too. For recommended tools and methods for speaking your book, please visit **NoWriting.PublishToSell.Com**. Please note you don't need to make a decision between writing and speaking, you can combine the two. I myself find that if I am having trouble writing about a subject, I can easily speak about it. The transcript becomes the basis for my writing, and keeps the momentum going.

> Whatever you do, you must DO. Don't "think about writing"—get words on the page.
>
> **Remember, write by the pound!**

Goodies

Goodies are the things you promised in your offers. After your manuscript is done, you'll want to turn your attention to creating them. Since these could be provided in a number of formats, including video and audio, we won't get too specific about what you should do. Just do it quickly. I also recommend sending the manuscript out to an editor before you start on the goodies. That way, the editing can begin while you're working on those.

If you get stuck, please refer back to the chapter on creating your offers (Brainstorm Part III: The Most Important Page In Your Book). We'll also cover how to use outsourcing later in the book, and you can find my most current advice on outsourcing at **Outsourcing. PublishToSell.Com**.

Finally, when your goodies are complete, you will want to revisit every place in the manuscript where they are referenced. When you first write the manuscript, you may only have a conceptual idea about the offers. Now that you have real content, you should revisit the manuscript to ensure that you are doing the best job of making your offers appealing.

What's the best thing you can do to enhance the offer pages selling your goodies? Specifically, tell the reader the benefits they will get from each. For instance, if you are using a video as a goodie, once you have recorded it, you should make sure that all the offers that reference it clearly state what readers stand to gain.

Illustrations
Illustrations are not necessary for most books. For some books, however, a few may be essential. Be sparing with illustrations, and when you use them, use the simplest illustration possible. Your goal is to explain, and simplicity and clarity are paramount.

Illustrations can make the production process more challenging, so keep in mind that you may require extra time to launch if you use them. To save time, it's best to work on illustrations while the manuscript is being edited.

As a rule of thumb, I recommend adding illustrations to the final layout only if you've got a highly polished manuscript and your readers are still confused about a concept. If your early readers love your book and you haven't shown them the illustrations you've created, then don't add them. You can probably find a use for the illustrations in other materials you produce for your business. Even if you never use them, just consider it a cost of doing business. Don't force them into the book if the reader doesn't need them.

Summary

- You don't need to write a perfect book, and you don't even need to write a good book—there are a million people with master's degrees dying to fix even the most messed up manuscript.

- Inventing a process is a critical to organizing your book, and making sure that you deliver a clear message to the reader. Please don't skip this step, which is detailed in the next chapter.

- If writing is a challenge on some chapters—or the whole book—then just speak instead of typing. For details and current tools for speaking your book, please visit **NoWriting.PublishToSell.Com**.

- The goodies are the things you promised in the offers you make in your book, and you'll want to schedule time for their creation. Create the manuscript *before* you spend time creating the goodies. You'll only create them after your editor has started working on the manuscript.

CREATE PART III

You Are Now an Inventor

To invent, you need a good imagination and a pile of junk.
~ THOMAS EDISON, RECORD HOLDER FOR U.S. PATENTS (1,093 OF THEM)

Whatever business you're in, you're about to become an inventor. I became an inventor when I wrote this book. You've already come across one of my inventions: The BCOOL Solution.

Why is inventing important for your manuscript? It helps clarify and persuade. You'll distill your process down to its basest essence, making it easy to understand. Furthermore, naming that process makes it proprietary; it's your intellectual property.

An acronym will make your method memorable. Examples such as KISS (keep it simple stupid) and FAQ (frequently asked questions) have become part of our common vernacular. Some are so deeply ingrained most people don't even know they are acronyms; for example scuba means self-contained underwater breathing apparatus.

How do you invent and name your own method? Here are the steps, which we'll go over in more detail:

1. Come up with the basic steps of your process. Just jot them down for your own benefit. Don't worry about how they sound.
2. Choose the power word in each step.
3. Brainstorm synonyms or look them up in a thesaurus.
4. Create a list of all the words and synonyms and highlight the first letter in each word.
5. Pick your favorite word from the letters on the list you created.
6. Write a few paragraphs explaining each step of the process.

I am going to do this right now before your very eyes. Indeed, I have already done the first step above—I just jotted down what I was thinking. So it's off to step 2.

Step 2 is rewriting each step in the process so that it starts with a power word. The power word is the most important word in the sentence. You'll have an opportunity to select alternative words in the next step, so don't worry about it being the perfect word. Just pick whatever is the most important word in that sentence and rewrite the sentence so it starts with that word. See below where I rewrite the steps above, leading with the power word:

1. Write the steps of your process
2. Choose the power words
3. Brainstorm synonyms
4. Highlight the first letter in each synonym

5. Cool word selection
6. Explain each step

So now we're on step 3, brainstorming synonyms. Where nothing interesting comes to mind, hit the thesaurus. You can take liberties here; this isn't English 101. If the word fits the context of your idea, add it to the list, even if it's not a literal synonym. Whenever possible, include some words that start with both vowels and consonants. If you have six steps and all your words are consonants, you'll have to go back to the drawing board.

1. Write—Draft, Compose, Author, Scrawl, Jot
2. Choose—Select, Pick, Anoint, Extract, Gather
3. Brainstorm—Think, Ponder, Contemplate, Research, Meditate
4. Highlight—Underline, Bold, Emphasize, Draw Attention, Sizzle
5. Cool—Power, Action (note that neither of these are literal synonyms, but they work for this step), Awesome, Amazing, Critical
6. Explain—Clarify, Define, Spell Out, Illustrate, Teach

That was easy, now on to step 4.

Write	Choose	Brainstorm	Highlight	Cool	Explain
Draft	Select	Think	Underline	Power	Clarify
Compose	Pick	Ponder	Bold	Action	Define
Author	Anoint	Contemplate	Emphasize	Awesome	Spell Out
Scrawl	Extract	Research	Draw Attention	Amazing	Illustrate
Jot	Gather	Meditate	Sizzle	Critical	Teach
↓	↓	↓	↓	↓	↓
Write	**Extract**	**Brainstorm**	**Bold**	**Action**	**Define**

Looking at the table above, I select:

1. **W**rite
2. **E**xtract
3. **B**rainstorm
4. **B**old
5. **A**ction
6. **D**efine

Thus, we get the acronym: WEBBAD

WEBBAD isn't so great. However, I like We Bad—*Stir Crazy* with Richard Pryor and Gene Wilder is one of my favorite movies (if you don't get the reference, watch the movie—it's hilarious). Thinking it over, I realize that Bold is a redundant step. It's reasonable to explain Brainstorming and Bolding letters at the same time, they don't need to be two steps.

So, voila! We now have five steps, and a better name. The process for inventing processes can be called: WE BAD

Boom! That's how it's done. Now to define each step. I did that above for illustrative purposes, but I'll do it again below so you have something to model when you do it.

The WE BAD Method of Invention

> **W**rite the steps of your process
> **E**xtract the power words
> **B**rainstorm synonyms
> **A**ction word selection
> **D**efine each step

Write the steps of your process
Begin by writing each of the steps involved in your process. Don't censor yourself. You'll whittle down the list later as needed. Each step in the process should be something meaningful. These are instructions that are meant to guide someone, but they're not meant to replace thinking. It's like reading a recipe; the recipe assumes you know certain things, like how to turn on the oven and measure a tablespoon of sugar. Make reasonable assumptions so your process doesn't become overly complicated. At this stage, each step should be described in one sentence, no more.

Extract the power words
Look at each sentence and determine the one word that drives that sentence—that is essential. That is your power word. Everything can be boiled down to one word. For example, consider of all the things that Google does. They have so much data and so many services it boggles the mind. And yet, the entire company can be summarized in one word: search.

Brainstorm synonyms
Not all words are created equal. Some words get people excited, motivated, and creative. Those are the words you want in your invention. Have fun with this, and keep brainstorming until you find words that excite you. They don't all have to be "A+" words. You can pick some words that are more steak than sizzle. If you have words that all begin with consonants, stretch to get a word or two that starts with a vowel. Also, don't be literal with your synonyms. This isn't a paper you'll be graded upon. Remember you're an inventor, you are supposed to be a little crazy and take liberties—enjoy!

Once you have your words, organize them into a list with your first-choice word at the top and synonyms below. Highlight or bold the first letter of each word in the table, so you can clearly see which letter you'll be using to create your acronym. Also, make sure you have at least four words in each column. If you have less, keep brainstorming.

Action word selection
Now that you've got a table full of words and you can see the letters from which you can choose, start to look for patterns. Try to come up with a word or words based on the first letter in each word. If you see a word or phrase that's really close but there's one extra step, then you may be able to consolidate two steps, as I did turning WEB BAD into WE BAD.

What if you don't like any of the words? First, you can try more brainstorming. Also, if you have some flexibility in the order of your steps, you can use an anagram solver to come up with some new words that may not have occurred to you. For example, take the letters from your process, and put them into an anagram solver (numerous sites can be found through Google). You'll get a list of words, and maybe you can make your process fit the word it provides. Try it a few times with different combinations of letters from your various synonyms and you will find something great. If not, look for more synonyms.

What if you still really don't like any of your words? If your process is only three or four steps, you don't have to choose a common word. There are a number of memorable short acronyms that don't even have vowels, for example WTF, LMK, TTYL, etc. Three or four letter acronyms are okay. If your acronym is longer than that, it's best to find a word or phrase to represent your method.

Define each step
This is where you elaborate on the do's and don'ts for each step in the process. Use examples whenever possible, and talk about potential

roadblocks and common mistakes. Ultimately, in your book, it's the 'define' portion that people will see. I'm only showing you more in this book because we are going "behind the curtain." So, in your book, these definitions each generally become a chapter.

For most purposes, a chapter will be somewhere in the area of ten pages. That's ten pages neat and pretty in a book, not ten pages of single-spaced type in a Word document. It's probably about 1,500 words, depending on your formatting. Of course, yours can be shorter or longer depending upon your business and your process. If you're in doubt, though, shoot for 1,500 words.

Warning!
Inventing your own process may seem unnecessary, and you don't have to use it in your finished product if you really don't believe it applies. You can also give it a name instead of using an acronym.

Yet you should do this exercise regardless of whether or not you use the process in your book. It will organize your thinking and compel you to think about things step by step. It also forces you to come up with synonyms, not just in the literal sense, but also more creatively, asking yourself what could substitute for this or that step?

Regardless of whether you intend to include your process in your published book, please create it. This will make your communication more clear, and it will help you with the next step: the very critical table of contents.

If you aren't fond of the name you've created, you can always revisit this process later, or brainstorm names with associates and friends. What's important for now is the step-by-step description that you've created. Until you have a clear vision of the "recipe" for what you're trying to communicate, it will be challenging to author a valuable book. Thus, as long as the steps are clear, you're ready to move on.

What if I get stuck?

Some people have trouble thinking in a linear, step-by-step fashion. There's no shame in that. If you fit that description, you probably are awesome at improvisation, and making magic without even knowing how it happens. Nevertheless, this exercise is critically important, so we'll have to push you to break through. There is a solution.

> *If you can't explain it to a six year old, you don't understand it yourself.*
> ~ ALBERT EINSTEIN, NOBEL PRIZE WINNING PHYSICIST

In the spirit of Einstein, you are going to clarify your process by explaining your business to a child. Speaking to a child forces you to say things simply, and to not leave out anything. When the child looks confused, you have to rethink and restate what you've said. Kids are brilliant at asking questions about all manner of things you haven't considered.

Record the conversation, and repeat with more children as needed. You'll probably have a lot of laughs doing this, and you *absolutely* will have some laughs listening to it afterward. It's a fun exercise that serves as a great tool.

Summary

- Don't be tempted to skip the steps in this chapter. Even if it feels unnatural—or *especially* if it feels unnatural—it's extremely valuable. If you can't define a step-by-step recipe for the reader, your book will not be well organized.

- You don't have to use the name you create with the WE BAD technique in your book. Call it anything you want. Doing the exercise and stimulating the thought is the critical part, not the name.

- If you are stumped when you start this process, then sit down with a child and explain to them what you do in your business. Record that conversation. Speaking with a child will force you to say things in simple terms, and kids are great at asking questions. You may have to repeat this process a few times, but it will help and be fun.

CREATE PART IV

The Mighty, Mighty Table of Contents

If you do enough planning before you start to write, there's no way you can have writer's block.
~ R.L. Stine, author of hundreds of novels

Once you have invented your own process, writing the table of contents becomes easy. You're about a third of the way done with the table of contents after completing the steps in the previous chapter. Each step of your process can be a chapter, or perhaps even more, as in *Publish to Sell*.

The next third of the process is noting the other things you may wish to discuss that aren't directly part of your process. Specifically, these are questions you will want to answer in every book, and hence plan for in the table of contents:

- *What's in it for the reader?*
  At least a couple of chapters should drill home the message of why the subject matter at hand can revolutionize the reader's life, their business, and/or their bank account. **You can never spend too much time talking about the two R's: Reader Results.** Always remember that results matter more than your credentials (or lack thereof), the features of your product or service, or anything else.

- *Why are you qualified to write this book?*
  Nobody wants to read a book by someone who doesn't know what they are talking about. Provide some evidence that you have real, battle-tested knowledge of this subject. Your proven results are all that matter here, not credentials. You're not writing a resume. Provide specific examples of your expertise, so it's clear that you're not writing from an academic or theoretical perspective.

- *Why is this book different from the 587 books that have already been written on this subject?*
  If your book isn't substantially different and better than what's already been written, then it has no purpose. Take a stand, explain what's been going on in the industry, and why it's time for this fresh, new perspective.

- *Who is right for this book? Who is wrong for this book?*
  You can't be all things to all people. Let's get the right people reading and the wrong people moving along.

There will be many other things that will come to you as you begin this process. Put them all in the table of contents. It's better to have too much than too little. You can always pare it down later.

The final third of the process is making the titles compelling. "Why I Am Qualified to Write This Book" may be the topic you'll discuss, but it's a boring chapter title. Do *you* want to read something with that title? "How I Made $70,000 by Accident" is the same exact chapter, but it's a lot more interesting.

You will be better positioned to rename your chapter titles after you have written your manuscript. So don't let this final step keep you from moving forward. Just get all the subjects into the table of contents, and plan to revisit it later to make the names more interesting.

If you get stumped at any time regarding the table of contents, just use these questions as chapter titles. If you see "What's in it for the reader?" at the top of the page, you'll have a lot to say. The exact title of each chapter isn't the critical part of the table of contents—your editor can help with that. What's important is to have enough subject matter, and some reasonable semblance of order, so that you can move through the writing and editing process quickly.

Three Silver Bullets

In the movies you only get one silver bullet to kill the super-villain. You're going to get a lot more here. Specifically, you will create three critical points for each chapter that you want to cover. Just one sentence for each (i.e. one bullet point). If you can come up with more than three, that's even better.

For example, let's examine one chapter that will be in every book: what's in it for the reader. You should have at least three points to make in this chapter. You'll summarize all the great benefits the reader will receive when they apply the information in your book. You will of course expand on these points in the manuscript. For now, you just want to know the outline of what will be in the manuscript.

Below are some silver bullets I created to answer this question for *Publish to Sell*. In other words, here are some things that authoring a book in the *Publish To Sell* style will do for you, the reader:

- Dramatically increase your income
- Make work more enjoyable
- Reduce stress
- Help your employees become more effective and happier
- Prepare clients to do business on your terms
- Clarify and improve your business strategy
- Sell more face to face, even to people that haven't read your book
- Make it easier to open global markets
- Multiply the effectiveness of existing marketing and sales efforts
- Leverage the multi-billion dollar Amazon platform
- Get consistent long-term results, and not be dependent upon inconsistent "roller coaster" marketing

As you can see above, I had a lot more than three silver bullets. So, I was able to expand the subject into multiple chapters. If you only come up with three, then you'll just have one chapter. Even if you only come up with a couple for any given chapter, more will probably pop into your mind over time. So get started on this, but don't spend too much time on any one chapter. Just keep moving, and revisit this with a fresh mind to fill in any blanks.

Summary

- Lousy Table of Contents = Lousy Book. It's that simple. You must have a solid foundation before you can build a house that will last.

- The wonderful news is that the exercises you've done will define the majority of the table of contents, if not the entire thing. No need to create something out of thin air. You'll be very well prepared.

- When in doubt, remember RR: Reader Results. What gets results for the reader? What is in the reader's self-interest? Focus on that, and you can't go wrong. It's all about the reader, not you or your products or services.

ORGANIZE

1. Find a subject you care about
2. Do not ramble, though
3. Keep it simple
4. Have guts to cut
5. Sound like yourself
6. Say what you mean
~ Kurt Vonnegut, author

I would like to honor Kurt Vonnegut's genius. You can throw out the majority of books on writing, put the six lines above on a Post-it note and be way ahead of the game. So, if you doubt yourself as you organize your writing and work with editors, just refer back to the Post-it.

There are four steps in the *Organize* process of the BCOOL Solution:

Editing

Hire an editor to give you the broad overview of your manuscript. Think of this as editing with a meat cleaver, not a scalpel. This is where you'll want to ensure what's in the table of contents is actually in the book, and vice versa. You'll also want to make sure that the contents are ordered correctly, in a way that someone else can understand. Just because it makes sense to you does not mean it makes sense to the reader.

The best person for this job will be a developmental editor who "gets" marketing. This person is a unicorn, so good luck with that. You'll almost certainly wind up with someone who hasn't mastered marketing. Their field of expertise is editing. So, take their advice with a grain of salt, since your mission and their talents may not be completely aligned.

You want the editor to let you know what makes sense and what doesn't make sense, what they can follow or not follow. You can and should ignore their value judgments on the relative merits of your advice. Your editor is not your market.

> Think of the editor as a mechanic, and you're about to buy a car. You want the mechanic to tell you whether the car will run. You don't want the mechanic opining about whether you can afford a sports car. Their sole job is to ensure you don't buy a car that is going to fall apart when you drive it off the lot.
>
> Your editor is there to make your message clear. The editor's opinion on your message is irrelevant if he/she isn't similar to your PI Clients.

Market Feedback

Now you are ready to get feedback from ideal clients or people who are very similar to your ideal clients. **Do not get feedback from people who are dissimilar to your PI Clients.** It can be tempting to get all the feedback in the world and take an attitude of "the more the merrier." This is opening Pandora's box.

You don't want to have doubts about your content, and people outside your intended audience may have the opposite perspective on the same material. You must always remember that we are willing—even eager—to repel the wrong people with our book. So don't muck it up by getting suggestions from the wrong people.

The only problem with getting feedback from your market is that it can be time consuming. After all, if a client is doing you a favor reading your book, you can't give them a hard deadline. You may try to bribe them to get it done in a timely fashion, perhaps inviting them to dinner on a certain date to discuss the book (your treat, of course). Alternatively, you could ask them to focus on just one or two chapters that are especially relevant to them.

If you have someone in your life who gets wind of your project and would have hurt feelings if you don't ask for their feedback, the best time for their thoughts is during the final manuscript phase. By that time, you'll already know what your market thinks and this additional feedback can't fundamentally alter the structure. If you let random people read your manuscript during this phase, you must read their suggestions skeptically. If they read the finished product and see their comments weren't incorporated, you can blame your editor.

Final Manuscript

You're in the home stretch—congratulations! You'll want a fresh set of eyes on your manuscript at this point, so hire a proofreader to read the manuscript. The ideal person for the proofreading job is almost certainly not the same as the person from the previous phase. The proofreader should be going through the book with a fine-tooth comb, so to speak. His or her job is to ensure that each sentence makes sense, and conveys the tone you want.

An important point to note here is that most proofreaders are obsessed with formal standards of academic writing. Most business authors want to comply with the rules of the English language just enough to seem competent, but also want to take liberties to make the language more casual and accessible. Whatever level of formality you want, you must have that conversation up front with your proofreader. Otherwise, you may wind up either with an ocean of irrelevant red ink on your draft, or a document that is too informal for your intended market.

You yourself want to have a fresh set of eyes, so do NOT read your manuscript while the proofreader has it. You've been up to your neck in this project, and the best thing you can do is to get away from it, so your brain has some time to decompress and take a different perspective. Let the proofreader do his or her thing, and don't think about the book for a couple of days. When the proofreader has given it back to you, read it again from start to finish with a clear mind. Make any tweaks you think are important, and then send it back for final proofreading.

You must promise yourself that when it comes back from the proofreader the second time, the manuscript is officially DONE. No book is perfect, and yours won't be the first. So, don't be tempted to edit indefinitely. By this point, you've gone through a lot to make it a quality book. You'll hear suggestions after it's in print, and some of those will make you smack yourself in the head and say, "Duh! How did we miss that?" That is okay. Put those items on your list of ideas for the second edition.

This book is about delivering PI Clients, not showing up Shakespeare. By the time you have reached this point, you DO have a manuscript that will accomplish the objective. Don't let perfectionism delay you. Remember the proverb, "the perfect is the enemy of the good."

Chapter Summaries

One important—and fortunately very easy—element to add to your final manuscript is a summary at the end of each chapter. Simply list bullet points containing key concepts the reader should take away. This is hugely valuable to the reader, and it doesn't take much time. If you don't feel like doing it, you can easily pay one of the people who edited or proofread the book to do it. They should be able to turn it around in a day.

Summary

- Think of the editor as a mechanic, and you're about to buy a car. You want the mechanic to tell you whether the car will run. You don't want the mechanic opining about whether you can afford the car.

- Getting feedback from people who are representative of the clients you want is critically important. Getting feedback from people you would never, ever want as clients is dangerous—it puts bad ideas in your head, and creates confusion.

- Some people won't read a chapter, they'll just skim it. You may be doing that right now. For those people, chapter summaries are especially valuable. Chapter summaries don't take much time after the final manuscript is done, so please be sure to do this—or hire someone to do this—before you release your book.

OUTSOURCE

Good leaders delegate and empower others liberally.
~ Colin Powell, former U.S. General and Secretary of State

Outsourcing is critical because you can't possibly have the skills to do all important tasks well. For example, a great editor is a much different person than a great cover designer. The good news is that there is an ocean of people out there for you to tap, and many are incredibly talented. The bad news is that there is an ocean of people out there, and some of them are incompetent and frustrating. So how do you separate the good from the bad? How much should you expect to pay?

This book is designed to provide valuable information that will be just as helpful and relevant in ten years as it is the day I wrote it. The fundamentals of writing a book that delivers PI Clients will be much the same in ten years. However, the world of outsourcing will undoubtedly be vastly different in one year, let alone ten.

To provide you with actionable, current information about outsourcing, I present the Outsourcing Guide for *Publish to Sell*. It provides current estimates for various services, designed to suit a range of budgets. It will also provide specifics on where my clients and I have found the best people, and tips that you can use to find your own. To get this free guide, please visit **Outsourcing.PublishToSell.Com**. As the world changes, the guide will be updated to reflect it. What follows herein is information about outsourcing that will endure.

Cover

It never ceases to amaze me what extraordinary quality one can get for a modest fee. Consequently, one should get many diverse covers designed instead of just picking one style. You can then put them up for a vote by friends, clients and people on any lists you may have (e.g. email, LinkedIn, Facebook, etc.).

Putting covers out for a vote is valuable for two reasons:

1. It proves what people think is more attractive, and prevents you from making a big mistake. For example, I was dead wrong last time I put out two covers for a vote. My hands down favorite lost horribly, receiving just 19% of the votes.
2. The act of engaging people with a vote creates anticipation for your book. You may get questions and suggestions that will help you in the editing process. You may also generate some business or referrals just from the awareness the voting process creates.

Whatever you do, don't just pick one cover that feels right and run with it. Doing "one and done" is a huge missed opportunity.

The most important thing you can do to be successful with your cover design is to compile a group of covers that the designers can

model. At the very least, you should have a crystal-clear concept and some photos or illustrations that convey the style you want. The most common mistake in self-published books is to have the covers be too busy. A cover will never look unprofessional if it has a clean, minimalist layout.

Take a look at the covers of books that have sold millions of copies, or that Oprah has put on her reading list. Model real bestselling books, not random e-books. While we aren't trying to write a bestseller, we surely want to take advantage of the research they've done and the money the industry has spent.

To get you started, I've put together a swipe file of noteworthy book covers to give you ideas. Just visit **SwipeFile.PublishToSell.Com** to view them at your leisure. For a current list of cover design resources, including where to hire designers, please download the outsourcing guide at **Outsourcing.PublishToSell.Com**.

Paperback Layout

The layout of your book should be, above all, easy to read. Don't allow fancy formatting to get in the way of making your book easy on the eyes.

We also want the layout to be congruent with the tone and objective of your book. For example, if you're a lawyer looking to generate six-figure corporate litigation clients with your book, then don't get too cutesy or too creative. However, if you are a freelance package designer, being too conservative with the book layout could be detrimental.

No matter who you hire to do your layout, they will require guidance. Describe the "vibe" of what you want and also define some characteristics you'd like to avoid. Nothing is more helpful than specific examples. So, when you are reading anything—magazines, newspapers, blogs, or books—save pages that resonate with you. Specific examples will eliminate a lot of wasted effort and frustration trying to verbally explain a visual concept.

The brass tacks of layout will change with technology. As of 2014, Amazon will tell you that you can just upload a Word document and you are all set for a paperback book through their CreateSpace platform. Unfortunately, that isn't the reality for the vast majority of authors. Amazon is wonderful, and they've done every writer a great service. I'm confident they will refine and enhance the publishing process every year. For the moment, though, it's not easy to get the desired result.

Consequently, you'll want to consider your page layout person one of your most important resources. Hire someone who has depth of experience producing books through the CreateSpace platform. Note Amazon will provide layout services for you. But, in my experience, you can hire someone independent who is very skilled for a reasonable fee. Importantly, you can dictate the terms with an independent, whereas Amazon's bureaucracy is inflexible. Explore several options, and remember that your page layout person is like a building contractor: the most expensive one you'll ever hire will be the one who gives you the lowest bid.

After you have finalized your print layout, ask your layout person to create a PDF version of your book. This should include not only the interior layout, but also your front and back covers. You're going to want to email this PDF to people, so ask your layout person to be mindful of the size when they produce the file.

Kindle

Fortunately, Kindle production is much simpler than print layout. So once your paperback layout is completely done, the Kindle part will be easy. The same person who handles your paperback should be able to do Kindle formatting for you. If not, there are thousands of experienced Kindle bookmakers who will do this quickly. In the entire production process, Kindle is the easiest part, and undoubtedly it will get easier.

There are also many alternatives to Kindle, most notably Apple's iBooks platform. Over time there may be many more. As of 2014, however, Amazon's Kindle is so far ahead of every other platform that it's just not worth the time and effort to publish on other platforms. If you were of the BS Mindset, then sure, you'd need to be on every platform. But you're not, so don't worry about it. You can always have your book produced on other platforms in the future. It's certainly a lot easier for someone to create a book on a new platform when you already have the book in print, as a PDF, and on Kindle.

Audiobooks

To do an audiobook properly is no small task. It's like recording an album in a studio. You can try to wing it yourself or do it on the cheap, but you'll end up with something that misses the mark. A better alternative is to reserve audio for your goodies. You can record an interview or podcast, and it is simple and it's effective.

The difference between a podcast and an audiobook is that people are used to the high production value of a professionally produced audiobook. So if you don't go to these lengths, then it won't seem right. It's like the difference between a home movie and a feature film. We don't expect home movies to have special effects and great editing. However if you showed a home movie in a movie theater, it would seem terrible because you're expecting much more.

My advice is to get your book out the door and start getting PI Clients. You can revisit the audiobook in a few months, and if you still want to do it, you can pay for professional production out of the profits from your PI Clients. You can even pay a narrator, if you don't like the sound of your own voice. For current resources, visit **Outsourcing.PublishToSell.Com**.

Goodies

The goodies you provide based on the offers in your book are critical to delivering value to your readers. The basic idea is simple:

Offer → Response → Goodie Delivery

1. You will make an offer in the book. That offer will be for compelling content that adds value above and beyond what is in the book.
2. Some readers will choose to respond to your offer. You will collect some information or require some action on their part. You may collect their email address, get them to join an online group, or any number of things that enable you to communicate with them in the future.
3. Deliver the goodie to the reader. Instant gratification of electronic delivery is optimal. Furthermore, once this is set up, it can continue delivering without any incremental effort on your part. My favorite goodie delivery tools are kept current at **Resources.PublishToSell.Com**.

In conclusion, remember that outsourcing changes constantly. There are new techniques and resources, and changes to the methods of distribution and production. Even the brief information in this chapter will probably look outdated quickly. To minimize "the dinosaur effect," I'm putting current information online for you, free, at **Outsourcing.PublishToSell.Com**. That guide will go into detail on each of the steps and make specific recommendations.

Summary

- There are so many talented people available to work on your book, it's amazing. The best way to reach them, and use their services, changes constantly with technology. For current information, please get your free Outsourcing Guide at **Outsourcing.PublishToSell.Com**.

- Paperback editions are wonderfully satisfying and they are great marketing tools. I strongly encourage you to create a paperback edition of your book, and not just limit yourself to electronic versions.

- Create valuable goodies that deliver upon the promises you've made in your offers. For the latest resources in delivering these goodies, please visit **Resources.PublishToSell.Com**.

LAUNCH

When you launch in a rocket, you're not really flying that rocket. You're just sort of hanging on.
~ Michael P. Anderson, astronaut

The focus of this book is closing sales with PI Clients by delivering tremendous value to them. By implementing the methods we've discussed thus far, you have a book that will deliver PI Clients. The final step is getting it into people's hands—so the book can do its work for you now, and for years to come.

Sell in Your Sphere

The low-hanging fruit is all around you. There are people in your sphere of influence who will perceive you differently after you publish your book. They don't even need to read it, just adding the title "author" to your list of accomplishments puts you in a different light. Everyone wants to know someone cool and interesting. Being an author is way cooler and more interesting than just about any title listed on a business card. It's cocktail conversation, it's something that people want to talk about—and word of mouth is powerful.

This is the point in time where a physical, printed book pays the greatest dividends. While e-books and Kindle books absolutely have their value, they are not optimal for reaching out to the people you already know. *If I am going to give you a gift, I want to be able to literally give you a gift, so it's in your hands and you can touch it.* If I send you an email with a link, it's just not the same experience. There is no cocktail conversation about an email.

So, the first thing that you'll want to do after publishing your book is **give signed copies to the following groups of people:**

- **Past clients and customers**
  These are the most likely sources of future business and referrals. They should get signed copies immediately after the book is complete. You will almost certainly get business quickly from just this step.

- **People who should do business with you but have not**
  You may know them socially or professionally, but for whatever reason, they just haven't connected to do business. There's no need to sell them. Instead, give them a gift! And if that gift happens to persuade them that you're the expert in your field, so much the better.

- **Influencers who can deliver PI Clients**
  There are certain people you may know, or have worked with, who have a client base that trusts them and could benefit from your expertise. For example, lawyers and accountants can be a great referral source for many businesses. You probably know lawyers and accountants, so give them signed copies.

Be sure to let them know that if they have clients who may be interested, you can arrange to get free copies for them as well. Depending on the referral source, how many copies they might need, and the geographic location, it may be appropriate to offer the printed copy to the referrer and electronic copies to their clients. For example, if the influencer has a large email list, maybe they would include the PDF version of your book in an email.

Your chapter summaries are extremely valuable here, because you can distill them down to a one or two page summary of your book, tailored to suit each particular influencer's audience. For example, I was approached by an attorney who wanted a Top 10 list based on one of my books for use in a presentation. He was happy to give me full credit and put my contact information in his presentation. Since I had the chapter summaries, it only took thirty minutes to provide him with a PDF that was customized for his presentation.

Far in advance of publishing your book, you should start putting together a list of everyone in each of the above categories. As you think about it, you'll start to think of more and more people over time. So, don't try to do this all in one sitting. Allow it to percolate. In time, you'll probably have an extensive list.

While giving your book away for free may be counterintuitive, it's actually a highly cost-effective way to market your business. For example, let's imagine there are 100 people total in the above categories. Your printed book on CreateSpace will probably cost less than $3 per book. With delivery, you may be at $300. That $300 will be the best money you could ever spend.

These folks will have your book for years to come, they will do business with you, and they will refer business. If you are selling high-value products and services, it doesn't take many PI Clients to turn this book into a very profitable project. Frankly, even if each book cost $30 to print, the results would still be compelling. The fact that printing is so cheap and easy is the cherry on the sundae.

Integrate with Existing Marketing

If you already sell high-value products and services, then you must already have proven marketing methods that work for you. It doesn't matter what methods you use—direct mail, online, email or smoke signals—you can leverage your existing marketing to get your book into people's hands.

Foremost, you want to build some anticipation for your book. Getting your existing clients to vote on the cover for your book is an easy way to get them actively engaged in the process. You will have people reaching out to you just from this step—before the book is even published.

Another extremely simple way to leverage your book before launch is to add an excerpt of the book to whatever marketing you're already planning. For example, if you have a monthly newsletter, presumably the topic of that newsletter overlaps with at least one of the chapters of your book. Simply take an excerpt of that chapter and incorporate it in the newsletter. This is synergy at its finest—you are improving the quality of your newsletter with the book, and building anticipation for the launch.

Once the book is published, get the word out through your existing marketing channels. You may wish to offer a bonus to everyone who buys before a specific date—for example, a webinar in which you answer readers' questions. You could also offer bonuses specific to buying a certain number of copies. A few months after the book is published and the dust has settled from your launch, you can also experiment with free book promotions on Kindle. This costs nothing and can revive conversation about your book.

Frankly, if you've done your homework selling to your sphere, you don't need to drive yourself crazy with this phase of marketing. Selling to your sphere is the meat, and integrating with your existing marketing is the potatoes. The beauty of the BCOOL Solution is that you don't need a highly complicated and expensive launch. Your return on investment will certainly increase with additional marketing and promotion. Nevertheless you should be able to surpass your target revenue for the project by selling to your sphere, and a few simple additions to your existing marketing.

If you are a Type A marketer and you want to go absolutely gonzo with your marketing, then you have my blessing. For the rest of us, happily, getting great results from the BCOOL Solution is pretty straightforward.

No List? No Marketing? No Problem

> *The best time to plant an oak tree was 30 years ago.*
> *The second best time is right now.*
> ~ ANONYMOUS

I have known some highly successful businesspeople who don't do any advertising at all. They sell face to face, or on the phone, and have never built any automated marketing processes. They don't have an email list, they don't have a newsletter, and it's pretty much all handshakes and phone calls.

If you fit into this category, there is great news: you should get absolutely phenomenal results from selling to your sphere. Clearly, you have great relationships, and that will pay dividends.

However, the fact that you are looking for new methods of marketing—which we know, because you are reading this book—means that it's time to start doing some things that you haven't done in the past. Specifically, you should start marketing based on systems.

You may have resisted this in the past because you see competitors with very large lists and think, "I could never reach that kind of size now. Joe Blow has a lock on this market." While your list may never reach the same size as people who started years before you, that doesn't matter. This is about revenue. This is about PI Clients. It's not about sending information to 100,000 email inboxes where it never gets read.

Now it is time for you to create marketing systems that will deliver new prospects and cultivate relationships. These systems will leverage your time and generate business far beyond the time you put into them.

The most tried-and-true method is the newsletter. Keeping in touch with people has value, and it's a high-leverage technique that works for just about any business. Furthermore, once you have used the BCOOL Solution to publish your book, you'll have a lot of information that you can immediately use in a newsletter. An email newsletter can be set up in a day, even by those who are not technologically savvy. Alternatively, you can outsource production and delivery of a print newsletter if that's easier or more appropriate to your market.

There are numerous other ways to do systematized marketing. It's a huge subject beyond the scope of this book. Nevertheless, I would never leave you hanging without a timely resource. So, to learn more about the marketing methods and tools I use and recommend, please visit **Marketing.PublishToSell.Com**.

In conclusion, I encourage you to experiment with as many methods of marketing and promotion as you wish. The greatest value of your book is that it lasts over time and remains valuable. You can leverage it in many ways, and **a campaign that you start a year after launch can be just as effective as it is a month after launch.** You may get invited to do an interview two years after you've published your book. That's an opportunity, and it's every bit as powerful as the day after your book was released. That is the advantage of the BCOOL Solution: it's about generating PI Clients, and you can do that consistently—without stress—for many years to come.

Summary

- Start with the low-hanging fruit: people you already know. Giving away a hundred signed copies of your book to friends, prospects, and current clients is the best return on investment you may ever see in your lifetime.

- Your existing marketing and sales efforts can be made even more effective by incorporating your book. Whatever you are currently doing—whether it's face-to-face sales, direct mail, or online—use your book. You can sell it or give it away as you see fit, or do different things for different marketing channels. The potential here is tremendous.

- If you don't have a list, you should build one. Even a very small list can yield numerous PI Clients, and thus bring in a lot of revenue. You may learn more about current methods for marketing at **Marketing.PublishToSell.Com**.

AFTERWORD

The Biggest Mistake You Can Make— and How to Avoid It

An error doesn't become a mistake until you refuse to correct it.
~ JOHN F. KENNEDY, U.S. PRESIDENT 1961-1963

The greatest regret I have in business is not writing my first book many years earlier. It is the reason I am so passionate about getting other business owners to take action and get their books *done*. I do not want others to struggle in business, especially when I know that struggle is often unnecessary.

This isn't an academic issue, this is about putting food on the table. I remember times when I didn't know how I was going to pay the rent. The anxiety was unbearable, it sucked the life out of me.

Not long ago, I walked into the grocery store and I remembered those terrible times. It was such a relief to feel how distant they were, and I thought to myself, "it's so amazing that I can buy whatever I want in this store. Absolutely anything!" I'll always be thankful that I don't have to add up every penny before I approach the checkout line. My first book was a huge turning point in leaving that past behind and moving toward a more prosperous and satisfying future.

If I hadn't written a book, the struggle would have continued much longer. I might still be struggling today. After all, how many business owners do you know who seem to fight the same demons month after month and year after year, without real progress?

Decisive action is required to make meaningful change. Fortunately, you have the tools at your disposal to make the process go so much faster and easier than it did for me on my first book. You don't have to stare at a blank screen and wonder what comes next. You just have to follow the plan, step by step, and you *will* be successful. Your life and your business *will* change for the better.

Your book will increase your revenue, but that's far from the only benefit. Your quality of life will improve—you'll be dealing with wonderful clients you enjoy, and who get great results implementing your advice. Your employees will do their jobs better, equipped with a complete vision of the business. Your strategy will be crystal clear, you'll have opportunities in new markets and the list of benefits goes on and on.

I have never, ever heard a business owner who has written a book say, "I wish I hadn't become an author." It simply never happens. The benefits are massive, and the only reason most people never author a book is because they don't have a plan and it seems too overwhelming.

Afterword

Fortunately, that fate won't befall you. I have done everything I can do to remove any obstacles and excuses. A book will absolutely improve your business and your life, and it is so much easier to create with the formula for success in your hands.

*So how can you possibly mess up the book,
now that you have this valuable, practical knowledge?*

Have you ever been, or are you now, out of shape? It's safe to say that you have long known two absolutely guaranteed methods to get back in shape: eat better and exercise more. And yet, you were/are out of shape, so what happened? Actually, it's what *didn't* happen that's the problem.

Knowledge can only take you so far—it's action that counts.

To get things done, people need accountability—someone or something to kick their behinds if they don't do what they're supposed to do. There are tools and services that can keep you on track, and they change often; a current guide is available at **GetItDone.PublishToSell.Com**. Please visit this site *immediately*, and take advantage of this free resource.

The single most important ingredient for success in any endeavor is action. That means taking action in the present, not "when you're ready" or "someday" but NOW.

Put the time on your calendar to make it happen. Whether you allocate 30 minutes or 8 hours per day, making time and working at it every day means it *will* get done. I encourage you to push yourself to get the most done as fast as possible to give you momentum. That momentum will carry you, and make the task so much easier.

Please put the next 10 minutes on your calendar right this very moment—and visit **GetItDone.PublishToSell.Com.** There you will find the best current resources and tools to keep you moving forward.

How many things in life have you intended to do, and then allowed years to pass by? It's simply too easy to put this incredible opportunity on the back burner, so please do not let it happen to you. You will not regret taking action. Your wallet and your sanity will be greatly improved by publishing a book using the methods you have read about here.

In closing, I hope you've enjoyed this book, and that you have great success and joy in your life as a result of what you've learned—and implemented. Your comments and success stories will be received most gratefully at **Contact.PublishToSell.Com.**

Thank you for reading.

Sincerely,
Alex

BONUSES FOR READERS

Throughout this book there have been many resources offered to readers. For easy reference, they are all listed below.

Recommended Tools, Websites, and Other Resources
Resources.PublishToSell.Com

Outsourcing Guide
Outsourcing.PublishToSell.Com

How to Be a Book Author Without Writing
NoWriting.PublishToSell.Com

Guide to Current Marketing and List Building Tools
Marketing.PublishToSell.Com

Swipe File of Book Covers You Can Model
SwipeFile.PublishToSell.Com

Personal Help With Your Book
Help.PublishToSell.Com

ACKNOWLEDGEMENTS

Foremost, I want to thank my parents, and my entire family, for their love and support throughout the years. I want to thank my beloved Tess for her encouragement and patience as I wrote and published this book.

Special thanks to Kevin Nations, it's no exaggeration to say that without your mentorship, *Publish to Sell* would never have been written.

I also want to give special thanks to Joe Polish, who was the inspiration for my first e-book, and set this whole wonderful adventure in motion. At the time, I had only met Joe once, and learned a tremendous amount just from the information he generously gives away. I'm now proud to call him a friend, and am grateful for him encouraging me on this path.

This book wouldn't exist without the people at Strategic Coach. Stephanie Song and Gina Pelligrini have taught me a great deal, and helped me enormously over the years. Dan Sullivan has inspired me, and his teachings permeate much of what I do on a daily basis. I'd also like to thank Jody McNamer for his honesty, encouragement, and help—he has made a great program even better.

Jonathan Cronstedt, Luke Fisher, John Hasson, Jessica Johnson, and Sameer Kumar deserve high praise for the brilliant insights they provided to improve a very rough draft. This book was dramatically improved by their help. I am so grateful to each of you.

Friends and colleagues who have encouraged me, inspired me, and helped make this book what it is today: Bob Acuff, Toren Ajk, Evan Algier, John Bailey, Tamara Bailey, Alex Barbara, Alex Changho, Suzanne Dibble, Mona Elesseily, Mark Evans, Morgan Giddings, Brian Horn, Nima Hakimi, Mitchel Harad, Andreas Hassellof, Jeremy Hermanns, Anna Hunter, Palash Islam, Iman Jalali, Jody Jelas, Robin Krigslund-Hansen, Mark Jamnik, Bari Lee, Max Lishansky, Adam Longfellow, Michael McDermott, Sarah Oberhofer, Bret Pacheco, Deborah Perzak, Nicholas Plummer, Stephanie Plumpton, Slaven Radic, Antonio Rillera, Derrick Reagins, Geoff Ronning, Simon Sakala, Jeremy Schoemaker, Scott Skinger, Jim Smyth, Maria Sparagis, Greg Spencer, Adam Strouse, Jonathan Volk, Jim Wang, David Wilson, John Wu, and Steven Yen.

I'd like to express gratitude for my Arizona friends, who've helped me through tough times, and cheered me through good times: Cassidy Amick, Mike Beck, Josh & Susie Berkowitz, Kevin Binkley, Blaine & Suzanne Black, Cheri Brady, Dick & Susan Burnham, Rick Cecala, Mike & Tricia Chen, Anisia Corona, Reed Day, Pat & Jackie Dukes, Melisa Fuentes Flaa, Nobuo Fukuda, Afra Lea Garcia-Corona, Chris & Tanya Gately, Matt & Farrah Greeson, Christopher Gross, Tami Higgins, KC Littlefield, Tom & Cindy McDonald, Layla & Kyle McDonough, Margaret McGuire, Jose & Claudia Menendez, Beth Mitchell, Dave Nerland, Jeff Nowak, John Orth, Bethany & Bre Parker, Frank & Toby Placenti, James Porter, Brian & Kacey Raab, Jaime Radow, Jim & Linda Saunders, Scott Scherger, Rheanna Schwan, Sabrina Sirianni, Kevin Stoddard, Sara Titterington, Siena

Acknowledgements

Tueros, Henrik & Teana Wagner, Josh Wertlieb, and Jock Wulffson. Thank you friends ☺

My life would certainly be much different without the friends I've made in Sweden. Also my life would be absent of some of my fondest memories if it weren't for: Sylwia Chaliss, Chris Hannell, Anna Kero, The Kyhlberg Family, Bjorn Lindgren, Sam Mesterton, Jonas Moller, Anne Øvsthus, Julie Nilson, Malin Persson, Richard Rosén, Malin Ruda, Robin Rutili, Thomas & Anna Svanstedt, Katarina Svensson, Bernhard Von Der Osten-sacken, Christian Wagner, Jenny Wiktoreng, and Nina Zandnia. Eternal thanks to Henrik Wagner for lugging me across the pond that first time, your native country agrees with me my friend!

Finally, I want to thank the clients who have found me through my books, and who have encouraged me to continue writing. It's been such a blessing to connect with like-minded people, and to be of service to you. I will respect privacy, but you know who you are. Thank you, thank you, thank you!

ABOUT THE AUTHOR

Alex Goldstein built a top real estate business at an unprecedented speed, in one of the most competitive markets in the U.S. This success came directly from publishing books to build a high value client base.

Today, Alex helps business owners grow their companies and improve their lifestyles. His methods have been used in numerous industries including law, financial services, consulting, marketing, and coaching.

Alex is an honors graduate of Northwestern University, and was also a visiting scholar at Oxford University. He is passionate about food and wine, having served on the boards of the International Wine & Food Society and the Confrérie des Chevaliers du Tastevin. He resides in Scottsdale, Arizona.

To contact Alex, please visit **Contact.PublishToSell.Com**.

CPSIA information can be obtained
at www.ICGtesting.com
Printed in the USA
BVOW06s2150020317
477659BV00001B/29/P